THE COMPLETE GUIDE TO GREYHOUNDS

Tarah Schwartz

Publication Data

Tarah Schwartz

The Complete Guide to Greyhounds – First edition.

Summary: "Successfully raising a Greyhound Dog from puppy to old age" – Provided by publisher.

ISBN: 978-1-954288-20-1

[1. Greyhounds – Non-Fiction] I. Title.

This book has been written with the published intent to provide accurate and authoritative information in regard to the subject matter included. While every reasonable precaution has been taken in preparation of this book the author and publisher expressly disclaim responsibility for any errors, omissions, or adverse effects arising from the use or application of the information contained inside. The techniques and suggestions are to be used at the reader's discretion and are not to be considered a substitute for professional veterinary care. If you suspect a medical problem with your dog, consult your veterinarian.

Design by Sorin Rădulescu

First paperback edition, 2021

TABLE OF CONTENTS

CHAPTER 1
The History of the Greyhound

The Origins of the Greyhound

The Greyhound is an elegant breed of hunting dog that likely descends from dogs owned by the ancient Egyptians and Celts. The earliest recognizable Greyhound went by the breed name *Vertragus*, which is a word of Celtic origin. *Vertragi*, the plural of *Vertragus*, were described as slim but powerful dogs with pointed muzzles and floppy ears. They were typically kept in large groups and were only released when the hunters' prey was in view. Their most common prey were wild hares, and the hunters would accompany the dogs on horseback.

Photo Courtesy of
Bianca King

These original sighthounds were so successful that a formal breeding program was eventually developed in the British Isles. By the 18th century, many of these dogs had recorded pedigrees in private studbooks, and by the 19th century, the studbooks were made public. All modern Greyhounds can trace their pedigrees back to these studbooks.

It is believed that the breed's name came from the Old English word *grighund*. The latter half of the word is the antecedent of the modern word "hound," but the exact meaning of *grig* remains lost to history. Etymologists don't believe that *grig* has any connection to the modern word "grey," but instead means something like "fair," based on the context the word is used in. This would explain why Greyhounds are called that despite not all of them being grey in color.

FUN FACT
Medieval Greyhounds

With their iconic silhouettes and overall popularity, it's hard to believe that these dogs may have nearly faced extinction several hundred years ago. However, thanks to members of the medieval English clergy who bred Greyhounds for the aristocracy, saving the canines from being wiped out during famine times, we can now enjoy the company of these beautiful dogs today.

The Greyhound and Racing

From the Middle East to the British Isles, nearly every geographic area has a native breed of sighthound. In the British Isles and continental Europe, these dogs were mainly used for the coursing of deer and hares. Once hunting was no longer necessary to feed the population, coursing became a sport, and dogs were run in competition.

As animal welfare became a priority, hunters were no longer allowed to use dogs to hunt prey like deer and hares. Rather than chasing an animal, modern-day Greyhounds competing in coursing or racing chase a lure similar to a windsock or white plastic bag. The artificial lure was invented by Owen Patrick Smith, an American who dreamed of ending the killing of jackrabbits and creating an industry around Greyhound racing as there is in horse racing.

The first recorded attempt at Greyhound racing was in 1876, but racing didn't actually gain popularity until the 1920s. By the 1930s, people were betting on dog races just as they were on horse races. The idea of an oval track and artificial lure quickly spread around the world. Greyhound racing quickly became an entertaining new sport with an opportunity for gambling.

Modern-day Greyhound racing has seen a significant decline due to concerns about the welfare of the dogs. It's estimated that between 2001 and 2011, gambling on Greyhound races in the United States declined by about 67%. As of 2021, only four Greyhound tracks remain open. There is one track in Iowa, two in West Virginia, and one in Arkansas, but the track in Arkansas is scheduled to close by 2022, and the track in Iowa faces a similar future.

Photo Courtesy of Hayley Lewis

Although state and local laws regulate the care of racing Greyhounds to some degree, each track has its own policies and procedures that Greyhound kennel owners and trainers must adhere to. All Greyhound racing in the United States is overseen by the National Greyhound Association, which is the primary registry organization in the country. Failure to comply to any of these regulations results in a ban from the sport. Despite these strict

Photo Courtesy of Viktória Glória Krucsó

regulations concerning the care of the dogs, Greyhound racing is under constant criticism from animal rights activists and is likely to end in the United States in the coming years. Greyhound racing continues to be a popular sport in other parts of the world.

The Modern Greyhound

The modern Greyhound is a beloved athlete and companion. There are two types of Greyhounds in the United States. The first type is bred for racing and registered by the National Greyhound Association (NGA). The second type is considered more of a show type, and these dogs are registered by the American Kennel Club (AKC). NGA Greyhounds are bred for the track and are typically retired between the ages of four and six. They are then passed on to rescue organizations that work to place the dogs in pet homes. NGA Greyhounds make up the majority of Greyhounds in the United States.

AKC Greyhounds are much rarer. In 2019, AKC ranked the Greyhound as the 162nd most popular breed out of 193 recognized dog breeds according to registration numbers. There is less of an industry surrounding AKC Greyhounds, so they don't have the numbers that NGA Greyhounds do. AKC Greyhound breeders and owners are a small but passionate group dedicated to the preservation of their breed.

There are some significant physical and behavioral differences between AKC and NGA Greyhounds that will be discussed in the next chapter. The physical differences are due to the different purposes the dogs are bred for, while the behavioral differences are due to the unique upbringing of racing dogs versus companion or show dogs.

CHAPTER 2
The Greyhound

Physical Characteristics

The Greyhound is an athletic yet elegant sighthound. At maturity, males typically weigh 65 to 70 pounds and measure 28 to 30 inches at the withers. Females generally weigh between 60 and 65 pounds and measure 27 to 28 inches at the withers. The overall appearance of the Greyhound should give the impression of speed and beauty.

According to the breed standard, the Greyhound's head should be long and narrow but still fairly wide between the dog's ears. The stop should be barely perceptible, and the muzzle should be long and powerful but not coarse. The ears of a Greyhound are small, thrown back, and folded. When the dog is excited, the ears are semi-pricked. A Greyhound's neck is long, muscular, and slightly arched, widening gradually into muscular shoulders.

The front legs of the Greyhound are perfectly straight, with strong pasterns and hare-like feet. The back is muscular and broad, and the hindquarters are wide and powerful. The abdomen should tuck up in the flanks. Like the front legs, the hind legs are straight with well-bent hocks and stifles. The Greyhound's tail is long, tapering, and has a slight upward curve to it.

The coat of the Greyhound is short and smooth. Greyhounds can come in any recognized color. According to the breed standard, the coat color is immaterial as the form and function of the dog should always come first.

Although the breed standard describes the American Kennel Club's ideal Greyhound, racing Greyhounds tend to be built differently. They are slightly smaller than show Greyhounds and are more heavily muscled. Their heads aren't quite as slender as those of show dogs, either. The main difference between the two types is in their behavioral rather than physical characteristics.

Behavioral Characteristics

In general, Greyhounds are even-tempered, gentle dogs. Though some can seem aloof toward strangers, they are extremely affectionate toward people they know and love. Well-socialized Greyhounds will tolerate strangers with no signs of fear or aggression, but they may be disinterested unless the stranger is carrying treats. Greyhounds can be sensitive, so without proper socialization, they can become fearful or nervous around new people, pets, or places.

Greyhounds are intelligent dogs, often compared to cats because of their independent nature. They are eager to please, but you may need to convince them to do as you ask. Greyhounds are incredibly sensitive dogs and do not respond well to harsh training. A stern voice is generally enough of a correction to stop a Greyhound from engaging in bad behavior. Although there are plenty of Greyhounds competing successfully in the obedience ring, they are not a breed that is easy to train. It takes patience and commitment, as well as a gentle hand, to train a Greyhound.

Some Greyhounds, especially ex-racing Greyhounds, can be prone to separation anxiety. This behavior is often due to the fact that many Greyhounds go their entire lives being surrounded by littermates or fellow racers, so when they are left alone for the first time in their new home, they may react badly. However, patience and training can improve or eliminate this behavior as long as it's applied consistently. Separation anxiety will be discussed in-depth in Chapter 8.

Show Greyhounds vs. Racing Greyhounds

When discussing Greyhounds, it's important to distinguish between the two main types: show-type Greyhounds and racing Greyhounds. Though both types have the same origins, differences have developed between them due to their distinctly different purposes. Show Greyhounds have mainly been bred to conform to the breed standard. They are slightly different in build and tend to be larger than racing Greyhounds. Most show-type Greyhounds are acquired from breeders rather than rescue organizations.

Racing Greyhounds were bred with the distinct purpose of running. Their athletic ability has been prized above all else, and as a result, they generally don't fit the breed standard as closely as their showline cousins. Racing Greyhounds are generally acquired by the general public from rescue organizations once they've retired from racing. There are also breeders that specialize in breeding Greyhounds for racing purposes, but the average racing-type Greyhound owner doesn't get their dog straight from the breeder.

Photo Courtesy of Blazka Ribic

Greyhounds as Family Dogs

Greyhounds can be excellent family dogs, especially with older children. They are calm, devoted companions that can be well-behaved around responsible children. However, Greyhounds are quite sensitive and will not respond well to rough handling or rambunctious behavior. This is particularly true of ex-racing Greyhounds, who may not have ever encountered a child before being placed in their new home.

FUN FACT
Greyhound Club of America (GCA)

The Greyhound Club of America (GCA) is the officially recognized national breed club for Greyhounds under the American Kennel Club (AKC). The GCA facilitates training and showing for the breed and promotes responsible breeding. For information about GCA events, or to catch the latest news, visit www. greyhoundclubofamericainc.org

Greyhounds have little fat or hair to protect them from the bumps or grabs of small children. Additionally, they tend to have rather thin skin, so rough handling can be painful or even injurious to them. They can be very sensitive and may react to inappropriate handling by biting. For this reason, it's important to teach children to behave responsibly around dogs, for their safety as well as the dog's. Once children are taught to respect their canine companions, Greyhounds are generally wonderful family dogs. As with all breeds, it's also possible that individual Greyhounds may prefer homes without children.

Greyhounds as Performance Dogs

Whether your Greyhound comes from a show breeder or a racing kennel, performance is in his blood. As such, many Greyhounds excel in a variety of dog sports. The most obvious choice of sport for any Greyhound is lure coursing. This is a sport specifically designed for sighthounds that involves a mechanically operated lure. Lure coursing is designed to simulate the experience of chasing live prey but in a safe and controlled environment.

Some Greyhounds also compete successfully in a variety of other sports, but success is generally dependent on each dog's independent aptitude, rather than the breed as a whole. While there are quite a few Greyhounds competing in sports such as agility, obedience, rally, or even dock diving, many Greyhounds would prefer to stay at home or participate in a more sighthound-friendly sport.

Greyhounds often compete successfully in sports such as Canicross or Bikejoring. These sports tend to be more popular in Europe, but they're catching on quickly in North America as well. Canicross requires the dog to wear a pulling harness, similar to those seen on sleddogs, which is attached to a belt around the handler's waist by a long leash. Other than the presence of dogs, Canicross competitions are run the same way as any other footrace, and distances and terrain vary by race. Bikejoring is similar, but instead of being attached directly to the handler, the dog is attached to a bicycle. Again, terrain and distances of Bikejoring races vary by location and competition. These sports appeal to the Greyhound's natural desire to run, but dogs with particularly high prey drives require quite a bit of training to prevent them from taking off after squirrels during competition.

Greyhounds and Prey Drive

Greyhounds were bred to hunt small animals, so it's only natural that the breed tends to have a high prey drive. For this reason, it's important to consider the Greyhound's natural desire to chase when deciding to bring one into a home with cats, small dogs, or other small pets.

Many Greyhounds may tolerate small animals well up until the moment they decide to run. Once the smaller animal starts to run, it may trigger the Greyhound's prey drive, and he may give chase, potentially injuring the smaller animal. It may require some training, but most breeders and

Photo Courtesy of Amy King

Greyhound rescues will have a good idea of each dog's prey drive so that they can find the right type of home. If you have small pets in your home, it's essential that you mention this to the breeder or rescue organization that you're working with so that they can match you to the right dog.

The Greyhound's natural desire to chase prey can also be a problem if they are allowed to run around off-leash in unfenced areas. If the area is secure, it's reasonable to allow a Greyhound some off-leash playtime, but if there is no fence, it could end in disaster. Once a Greyhound starts chasing its prey, your shouts and recall commands will be ignored. Greyhounds chasing prey can be so focused on the hunt that they may run into streets or other dangerous situations without even noticing. For this reason, Greyhounds must always be leashed when not in a securely fenced area.

Is the Greyhound Right for You?

Greyhounds are wonderful dogs, but they aren't right for everyone. They are a gentle and sensitive breed that can adapt to most lifestyles, but they do have specific needs. It's a common misconception that Greyhounds, especially ex-racers, are hyperactive or need a lot of room to exercise. The opposite is actually true. Greyhounds do not need large houses or yards and can do well in an apartment as long as their exercise needs are met. As with every breed, they need physical and mental stimulation daily to prevent boredom-related bad habits from developing.

As previously stated, Greyhounds are athletic and can be polite and well-behaved dogs, but if you're expecting an obedience competition star, you may want to consider a different breed. Greyhounds are independent by nature and may not always feel like listening to your commands. Additionally, off-leash competitions can be risky if your Greyhound catches sight of a small animal that he wants to chase. If you're looking for a gentle and athletic companion with no expectations of obedience ring success, the Greyhound may be the right dog for you.

Some Greyhounds, especially those coming off the track, may be prone to separation anxiety. These dogs are typically surrounded by other Greyhounds and their caretakers around the clock, so moving into a new home with periods of isolation can be frightening to them. If you're expecting your new Greyhound to immediately adapt to life in a pet home, you may need to reconsider your decision to adopt. Whether you get your Greyhound from a breeder or rescue organization, there's going to be a period of adjustment that you'll need to work through. Patience and consistent training will pay off. If you're willing to take the time to train your Greyhound and make him comfortable in his new surroundings, you'll be rewarded with a lifetime of love and companionship.

CHAPTER 3
Getting a Greyhound from a Breeder

Purchasing from a Breeder

Once you've decided to bring home a Greyhound, you'll need to decide if you want to adopt an ex-racer or purchase a dog from a reputable breeder. When making this decision, you'll need to consider your long-term goals for your new dog. If you're simply looking for an active family companion, you may be just as happy with a rescued Greyhound as you would a dog from a breeder. However, if you're looking for a conformation prospect that will turn heads in the show ring, a reputable breeder will be your best bet. If you're looking for a dog to compete in a specific sport with, a rescued

Greyhound may work for you, but a breeder who also competes in that sport may be better able to provide you with the dog of your dreams.

It's a common misconception that breeders only have puppies available, but many reputable breeders have adult dogs available from time to time. If you're not sure you want to deal with the challenges of raising a puppy, consider looking for an adult dog. Adult dogs from breeders are often retired show dogs or dogs from past litters that have been returned to the breeder. Most breeders have clauses in their contracts stating that if an owner can no longer care for their dog, it should be returned to the breeder. If that happens, the breeder may be looking to place the dog in a new home. There are also adult Greyhounds that have been retired from the show ring, and rather than incorporating the dog into their breeding program, a breeder may seek a pet or sport home for it.

You should also consider what gender you'd prefer your ideal Greyhound to be. While many owners are indifferent to the gender of their dog, if you have other pets in your home, they may have a preference. Greyhounds are not prone to same-sex aggression, but many other breeds are. If you already have a dog that is aggressive toward dogs of the same sex, you will want a Greyhound of the opposite sex. Some Greyhound owners report that females tend to be a bit more independent than males, but this is not true for every individual dog. Each Greyhound has its own personality, so if you or your current pets do not have a preference, the breeder you work with will have more options in matching you to the right dog.

Choosing a Reputable Breeder

Not all breeders have the same goal in mind. Reputable breeders care about their dogs as individuals as well as the breed as a whole. They seek to better the breed with every generation. Backyard breeders, on the other hand, usually only care about the money.

The first place to start your search is at a local dog show or sport competition. If you plan on competing in a specific sport with your Greyhound, head to a local competition and look for Greyhound handlers. Most people are more than happy to talk about their dogs, but be sure to do so while they're waiting for their turn rather than as they're headed into the competition ring. By watching these dogs in action and getting to know them through their handlers, you'll be able to get a good idea of what kind of dogs are being produced by certain breeders. Asking the handlers where they got their Greyhounds will help you find a breeder you're interested in, or you may decide to avoid that breeder based on what you see in their dogs.

FUN FACT
Greyhounds in the White House

Greyhounds are noble dogs and have been members of some of the greatest families in history. As of 2019, three Greyhounds have been presidential pets. John Tyler, the tenth president of the United States (1841–1845), owned an Italian Greyhound named Le Beau. The nineteenth president (1877–1881), Rutherford B. Hayes, owned a Greyhound named Grim, and the twenty-eighth president (1913–1921), Woodrow Wilson, owned a Greyhound named Mountain Boy.

If you don't have any shows or competitions near you, you can also contact the national breed club, or a local breed club, if you have one. The Greyhound Club of America, as well as local breed clubs, will be able to provide you with a list of reputable breeders. These clubs maintain a list of breeders that are active in the breed community and have a reputation for producing stellar dogs that adhere to the breed standard. Though you'll still need to ask plenty of questions to determine if the breeder is right for you, it's a good place to start.

Finally, the American Kennel Club has a section of their website called the AKC Marketplace. On the AKC Marketplace, you'll be able to search listings by breed, as well as gender if that matters to you. You'll be provided with a list of available Greyhound puppies, as well as listings for future litters. The listings will tell you if the breeder is a member of their national breed club or specialty club and if their dogs compete in AKC events. You'll also be able to see if the breeders perform applicable health tests on the sire and dam, as well as if they provide a health guarantee or are willing to take the puppy back if you can no longer care for it. In many cases, the listings will also tell you how many puppies are available, how old they are, and their price. If not, you'll need to contact the breeder directly for this information.

Questions to Ask Before Bringing a Greyhound Home

Once you find a breeder you're interested in, you'll need to ask specific questions to make sure they can provide you with your ideal Greyhound. The most important questions to ask are regarding the health test results of the sire and dam. If the dog you're interested in is over two years old, he or she may also have undergone rigorous health testing.

The Orthopedic Foundation for Animals (OFA) is one of the leading organizations in canine genetic research. Their Canine Health Information Center (CHIC) contains a database of health results for thousands of dogs of each and every breed. The OFA recommends specific tests for each breed based on what conditions are common for that breed. For Greyhounds, the OFA recommends a cardiac evaluation performed by a board-certified cardiologist. Greyhounds must also participate in the OFA/CHIC DNA Repository, so a blood sample submission is required. All dogs, regardless of breed, need to be permanently identified by tattoo or microchip before the OFA will make the results publicly available.

A reputable breeder will be able to provide you with their dogs' CHIC numbers so that you can see their results on the OFA website. You can

Photo Courtesy of Clair Cuthbertson

also search the website with the dogs' registered names. A less reputable breeder will not provide you with this information as they likely haven't had appropriate testing done on their dogs. They may claim that the dogs have been examined by a vet and determined to be healthy, but this is not the same as health testing. Be sure to ask specifically about OFA/CHIC records.

In addition to asking about health testing, here are a few questions to ask your breeder:

- What vaccinations has the dog received?
- Has the dog been dewormed?
- Has the dog itself undergone health testing?
- What titles have the parents earned?
- Have puppies from past litters earned titles in conformation or other sports?
- Does this dog have the potential to succeed in conformation or other sports?

If you aren't looking for a Greyhound to compete in shows or competitions, the last few questions may not apply to you. However, you should ask the breeder about the temperament and personality of the dog you're interested in. If you're working with a reputable breeder, they'll likely have just as many questions for you as you do for them, so they can match you to the right dog. If the Greyhound in question is an adult rather than a puppy, there are also some age-specific questions you might want to ask:

- Why is the dog being rehomed?
- How is the dog around children?
- What kind of prey drive does the dog have?
- Is the dog safe around small pets like cats?
- Is the dog fully housetrained?
- Has the dog been spayed or neutered?
- Can you show me the dog's performance record?
- Does the dog have any behavioral problems or bad habits?

You should also ask about what type of food the breeder feeds his or her Greyhounds. This may not impact the diet you intend to feed your new dog, but you should feed the dog his current diet for at least a few days after bringing him home before slowly transitioning him to the food of your choice. This will help ease stress-related digestive problems and prevent problems from changing food too quickly. Don't forget to ask about food allergies, sensitivities, and preferences.

Photo Courtesy of Nicole Becker

Contracts and Guarantees

When you purchase a Greyhound puppy or adult from a reputable breeder, you're probably going to have to sign a contract before you are allowed to bring the dog home. Contracts are legal documents that are designed to protect both you and the breeder financially while also prioritizing the wellbeing of the dog. The contract will specify which Greyhound you're buying, the purchase price, and any guarantees or conditions of the purchase.

By signing the contract, you're agreeing to take on the responsibility of the Greyhound in question. This means that you will be required to provide him with regular veterinary care and spaying or neutering if required. If you're buying a Greyhound as a pet or sport prospect, spaying or neutering may or may not be required by the breeder. However, dogs competing in conformation must remain intact, so your contract may have different requirements if you're buying a show prospect. Some breeders may also refund a portion of the purchase price once you provide proof of spaying or neutering.

Some breeders will also specify what type of food they want you to feed your new Greyhound. Many breeders have decades of dog experience and have learned through trial and error which types of food suit their dogs best. Breeders that feed their Greyhounds a raw diet may prefer that their puppies go to a home that will continue feeding them raw food.

The contract will also have a section regarding the breeder's obligations. This may include a health guarantee against genetic disorders common to the breed. Reputable breeders test for these disorders to eliminate them from the gene pool, so the risk of a puppy developing one of these health problems is generally low anyway. However, should a puppy or adult Greyhound develop a serious health problem, the contract should state what will be done about it. Most breeders will gladly accept the dog back, but it may be that the owners will be allowed to keep the dog if they've already fallen in love with it. If the dog passes away due to the genetic disorder, the contract may also state whether the owner is entitled to a refund or replacement puppy.

Most breeder contracts will also state that the breeder will take the Greyhound back at any time in its life for any reason. Many breeders will take the dog back with no questions asked, as the dog's wellbeing is always their priority. This is to prevent the dog from ending up in an inappropriate home or shelter.

Remember, no two breeders will have the same contract, so it's crucial that you read the contract in its entirety and discuss it with the breeder if necessary. This is a legally binding contract, so any questions or concerns need to be discussed before you sign. Reputable breeders are always transparent in their actions, so don't feel shy about asking. They want you to make sure their dogs are going to the right home, so you should always feel comfortable asking the breeder questions about the dog or contract.

How to Choose Your Ideal Dog from a Breeder

Many potential Greyhound owners are nervous about whether they'll be able to choose the right dog for their lifestyle. When buying a puppy or adult from a reputable breeder, this should not be a concern. As long as the breeder has thoroughly interviewed you and you've been honest about your goals and living situation, he or she should be able to match you to the right dog. Remember, breeders know their dogs better than anyone, so as long as you've been honest, they should be able to find you the perfect Greyhound.

In fact, many breeders will not allow you to pick the puppy yourself. It's common for puppy buyers to get caught up in a puppy's appearance or personality without considering what the dog will be like as an adult. To prevent buyers from taking home a puppy with too much energy or the wrong level of drive, breeders will choose your puppy based on the needs and wants that you've already discussed. Even if you are given a choice between puppies, you should still consider the breeder's advice.

CHAPTER 4
Rescuing a Greyhound

Why Rescue a Greyhound

As with any other rescue dog, by rescuing a Greyhound, you're providing a home for a dog in need. Once Greyhounds retire from racing, racing kennels are generally not equipped to provide for the dogs for the rest of their lives, so they are passed on to rescue organizations. These rescue organizations then match the dogs to their new homes. By rescuing a Greyhound, you are supporting the organizations that take care of these dogs after their racing careers have ended.

Rescue organizations that take in ex-racing Greyhounds generally accept the dogs from their contacts at tracks across the country. They then provide the dogs with any veterinary care they may need. This may range from the

Photo Courtesy of Pam Triplett

treatment of an injury or illness to basic vaccinations or deworming. Spaying and neutering are often done shortly after intake as well. If the Greyhounds need grooming, they are given a good bath and brushing. The majority of these organizations are also foster-home-based, so the dogs get to experience living in a home before they are put up for adoption. The fee you pay for adopting a Greyhound goes toward helping these organizations continue to care for dogs in need.

Contrary to what many believe, Greyhounds are not abused at racing kennels. Their handling is more often utilitarian, with straightforward treatment related to their training. Though there are exceptions to every rule, most Greyhounds are treated with respect during their racing careers. Proof can be seen in most Greyhounds' friendly and positive outlook toward people. If they were abused, they wouldn't be so eager to receive attention from their favorite humans. They are also treated as athletes, because as with most athletes, if they aren't taken care of, they won't be able to perform well. Rescued Greyhounds are typically in peak physical condition when they are taken in by rescue organizations. Most Greyhounds are given up to rescue organizations when they are no longer fast enough to win or if they are injured. Though there are some Greyhounds that are taken in by rescues from abusive situations, the vast majority are well taken care of.

Greyhounds in Rescue

Greyhounds coming from a racing background differ from other types of rescue dogs in that their history is well documented. This is helpful in knowing what to expect from a rescued Greyhound.

During their racing career, Greyhounds will rarely meet any other type of dog and do not encounter cats or children. Because of this, Greyhounds may or may not react differently toward dogs of other breeds. Despite their lack of experience outside other Greyhounds, they are generally quite sociable toward other dogs and rarely show aggression. Racing Greyhounds are crate trained and usually find comfort in the safe space of their kennel.

One of the most common challenges owners face with rescued Greyhounds is separation anxiety. Remember, racing Greyhounds are constantly surrounded by many other dogs, so if they come into a new home with no other dogs, or even one or two, they may display inappropriate behavior when left alone. Additionally, they often have anxiety surrounding their new state of unemployment. Greyhounds are used to a routine and having a job, so when their schedule is changed, and they no longer have that job, their anxiety is often expressed as separation anxiety. Thankfully, with patience, training, and a consistent routine, most Greyhounds can quickly adapt to life off the track.

Greyhounds can also be quite nervous in new environments. Things like stairs, slick floors, mirrors, and household noises can be frightening to a Greyhound that has just left the track environment. Most rescued Greyhounds spend time in a foster home prior to adoption so that they have time to get used to these things, but it's important to understand that your Greyhound may react with fear to things that you view as everyday objects. However, Greyhounds are people pleasers that respond well to positive reinforcement, so with consistent training, they can get used to new environments quickly.

QUOTE

"I feel like people have a lot of misconceptions about rescue dogs. Like 'oh, someone threw it away; there must be something wrong with it'—but I really enjoy taking people's throwaway animals and making them into something great."

Samantha Valle,
owner and trainer of a world-record-holding Greyhound named Feather

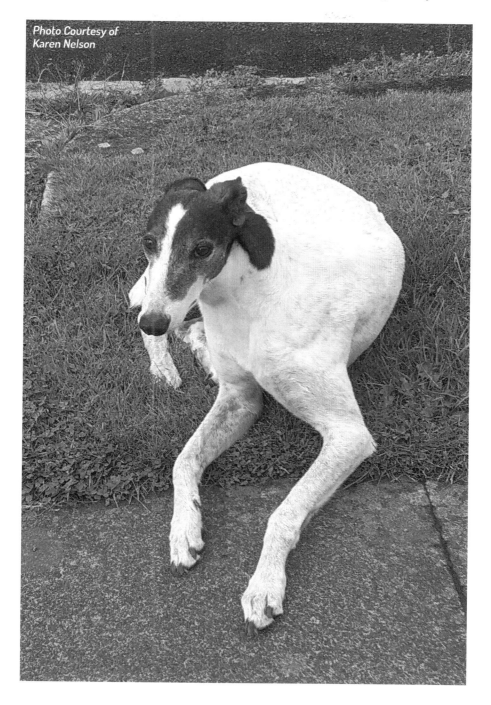

Photo Courtesy of
Karen Nelson

How to Find a Reputable Rescue

As with buying a dog from a breeder, it's important to do your research and find a reputable rescue. Just as with breeders, there are rescues that are more interested in the money than the welfare of the dogs in their care. Reputable rescues ensure that animals are given all necessary medical care and are placed in loving foster homes until they can find their forever homes. They also temperament test all dogs to make sure they're going to the right home. With Greyhounds, it's crucial that all dogs are tested with cats and children to make sure they don't go to homes where they may become a liability.

Reputable rescues often have strict adoption requirements and a lengthy application process. This may feel frustrating, but it's essential in ensuring the Greyhounds go to the right home. Otherwise, they risk being returned to the rescue, which can be stressful and confusing for the dog. You may also need to provide references such as friends and family or your veterinarian. As with reputable breeders, most rescues also require you to return the dog to them if you can no longer provide care for any reason.

Reputable rescue organizations operate as legal 501(c)(3) non-profit entities. Reputable rescues are also often recommended by other local, established rescue organizations. You may even be able to contact other rescues if you would like references from the organization you're consider-ing adopting from.

Reputable rescues also often provide support to adopters after they take the dog home. Though not all organizations have the resources for this, many will allow you to call and ask questions if needed. This is often the dif-ference between dogs finding their forever homes or being returned to the rescue. While this shouldn't be a requirement in your search for a rescue, it is a sign of a reputable organization.

Questions to Ask Before Adopting a Greyhound

When rescuing a Greyhound, you'll likely need to fill out an extensive application asking about every aspect of your lifestyle that applies to dog ownership. The rescue organization will get to know you, but you'll need to take responsibility for asking about the dog in question to make sure you feel confident in your ability to provide for that dog. If you don't ask the right questions, you may be matched to a Greyhound that isn't quite suited to your lifestyle. These questions will also help you determine whether an organization is reputable or not. Questions to consider asking rescue staff or volunteers include:

- What is the dog's temperament like?
- Has the dog ever shown aggressive behavior?
- Is the dog overly fearful?
- Does the dog tolerate dogs of other breeds?
- Is the dog cat-friendly?
- What is the dog's prey drive like?
- Is the dog safe around smaller dogs?
- How is the dog around children?
- Is the dog fully housetrained?
- Does the dog have any known bad habits or behavioral issues?
- What type of food is the dog eating now?

Though reputable rescues will have taken care of their Greyhounds medical needs, it's important to ask anyway. If the dog is new to the rescue, it may not have completed its recommended treatments yet, so the information may be relevant to how soon you can take the dog home. Medical questions to ask include:

- Has the dog been spayed or neutered?
- What vaccinations has the dog received?
- When was the dog last dewormed?
- Was the dog retired from racing due to an injury?
- If so, what is the dog's prognosis?
- Has the dog had any known health problems in the past?

If at any point the rescue organization avoids answering certain questions or doesn't seem like they're telling the truth, you're likely not working with a reputable rescue. Reputable Greyhound rescues will always be completely transparent about their dogs. If the person you're speaking to seems sketchy or dishonest, they probably are. Though it's easy to feel bad for the dogs in their care, it's important to avoid supporting these rescues. Without the income generated from adoption fees, these rescues will go out of business, leaving more room for rescues who actually care about the welfare of the Greyhounds in their care.

*Photo Courtesy of
Kennedy Vance*

How to Choose Your Ideal Dog from a Rescue

When you look at a rescue organization's website or attend a local adoption event, it can be easy to become infatuated with a specific Greyhound based on your immediate impression or the dog's appearance. Everyone finds different colors or markings appealing, but it's crucial that you choose your dog based on his or her personality and suitability for your lifestyle rather than appearance.

Additionally, by the time you complete the adoption application and screening, that specific Greyhound may have already found its forever home, so it's important to remain open-minded. As long as you're honest in your application, the rescue will be able to help match you to your ideal dog. If you have any dealbreakers in terms of appearance or behavior, be sure to mention them to rescue staff or volunteers. The more they know about you, the better they'll be able to find the right dog for you.

You'll also need to consider your goals for your new Greyhound. If you're just looking for an active companion, you may have more options to consider, but if you're rescuing a Greyhound to compete within a certain sport, you'll need to look for a dog with the right traits to succeed in that sport. Not all dogs are suitable for all sports, so knowing what you're looking for will help you narrow down the field.

You may find yourself waiting for the right dog to come into rescue, but if you've already filled out the application and completed the screening process, you should be able to be approved for adoption more quickly once you meet your perfect Greyhound. You might also consider fostering a Greyhound if you aren't yet sure about adoption. Fostering is a great way to get to know a dog and provide it with a loving home without the commitment of caring for it for a lifetime. You might just have your first "foster fail" and end up adopting the dog after all.

CHAPTER 5
Preparing Your Family for a Greyhound

Yearly Costs of Owning a Greyhound

Whether you're adopting a Greyhound from a reputable rescue group or buying one from a breeder, it's crucial to understand the financial responsibility that you're about to take on. Bringing a new dog home might not seem like a big deal, but the yearly cost of dog ownership is frequently much higher than many people expect. However, with proper financial planning, dog ownership is possible for most families and individuals.

The first cost that you're likely to encounter with your new Greyhound is the adoption fee or purchase price. Generally, rescuing a dog will be less expensive than buying from a breeder, but you should still expect to pay several hundred dollars. Most organizations charge between $250 and $500.

Remember, your adopted Greyhound will likely have received all vaccinations and has been spayed or neutered during his time with the rescue organization. His adoption fee will go toward covering the cost of his veterinary care, so even if the adoption fee seems high, it's important to understand the value.

If you're working with a reputable Greyhound breeder, you're going to pay a much higher price than if you choose to adopt from a rescue organization. Most pet-quality AKC

HELPFUL TIP
Poison Preparedness

Due to the low body-fat percentage of most Greyhounds, this breed is more sensitive to medication, anesthesia, and toxins. If you notice or suspect that your Greyhound has encountered a toxin, you can call the ASPCA Animal Poison Control Center (888-426-4435) or the National Animal Poison Control Center (1-900-680-0000). Fees may apply. Signs that your Greyhound has been poisoned include difficulty breathing, digestive changes, increased urination, convulsions, and more.

registered Greyhounds cost between $1,000 and $2,000. If you're looking for a show or sport prospect, you may be looking at spending upwards of $2,500. Puppies purchased from breeders typically have at least one round of vaccines and deworming, but the cost of spaying or neutering and the final rounds of vaccinations will be your responsibility. Though the initial cost of a Greyhound from a breeder may be higher, if the parents have been thoroughly health tested, you can be sure that your new dog will have as healthy of a life as possible.

The initial cost of your Greyhound isn't the only cost within the first few months of ownership. You'll also need to budget for basic supplies and routine veterinary care. If you have other dogs in the home, you may already have many supplies on hand, but if this will be your only dog, you'll need to prepare. Depending on where you live and what type of supplies you choose to buy, you should expect to pay between $1,065 and $3,810 during the first year with your Greyhound. Again, this is not including the initial cost of the purchase price or adoption fee.

Here is a basic breakdown of potential costs within the first year of Greyhound ownership.

Mandatory Expenses	Cost Estimate
Food	$300 - $900
Food and Water Dishes	$10 - $50
Treats	$50 - $150
Toys	$20 - $100
Collars and Leashes	$10 - $100
Crate	$50 - $200
Dog Beds	$50 - $350
Vaccines and Routine Veterinary Care	$150 - $500
Heartworm Testing	$10 - $35
Heartworm Prevention	$25 - $125
Flea and Tick Prevention	$40 - $200
Spaying and Neutering	$150 - $600
Puppy Classes	$200 - $500
Total	$1065 - $3810

Though the previous table includes most of the costs you'll face in the first year with your Greyhound, it doesn't include everything. Greyhounds have short coats that require little grooming, but if you aren't willing or able to bathe your new dog and trim his nails, you'll have to arrange for a professional groomer to do it. Depending on where you live, expect to pay between $40 and $80 per groom. The cost may be higher if you hire a mobile groomer to come to your house rather than taking your Greyhound to them.

If you're a frequent traveler, you'll either need to bring your Greyhound with you or make arrangements for him to stay somewhere while you're gone. Whether you choose a pet sitter to come to your home or a boarding facility, you'll need to add the daily cost of your dog's stay into your budget. Depending on where you live and the quality of care you expect your dog to receive, expect to pay around $50 per day.

The highest cost you may face as a Greyhound owner is emergency veterinary care. Though you will obviously do your best to keep your dog healthy and injury-free, accidents and illnesses can and do happen. Emergency care can range from just a few hundred dollars to several thousand or more. Surgeries, specialty veterinary care, and hospitalizations can be expensive. Some owners choose to protect their Greyhounds with pet insurance, while others set aside a monthly lump sum to save for a rainy day. Whether or not pet insurance is right for you and your Greyhound is a personal choice, but it will be discussed in more detail in Chapter 17.

Photo Courtesy of
Nina Fossard

Possible Expenses	Cost Estimate
Professional Grooming	$150 - $900+
Emergency Veterinary Services	$200 - $2000+
Pet Sitting or Boarding	$15 - $80+ per day

These estimates can seem frightening, but they are not intended to discourage you from bringing a Greyhound into your life. It's just import-ant to consider the potential cost of dog ownership. Welcoming any animal into your home is a big responsibility, so you need to make sure that you're prepared so that you can give your new family member the best care possible.

Preparing Children

Children and dogs can be wonderful companions, but only with a proper introduction and appropriate guidelines. Before you can bring your Greyhound home, you need to discuss your new family member with your children and teach them the rules of interacting with a new dog. Even if you have other pets in the home, a new dog can be an exciting time, and you'll need your children to behave appropriately so as not to frighten the new addition. A nervous Greyhound in a new environment could lash out if it perceives overly enthusiastic children as a threat, so it's best to have a thoughtful discussion about the do's and don'ts of interacting with an unfamiliar dog.

Whether you're bringing home a puppy or an adult Greyhound, the basic rules will be the same. You'll need to explain to the kids that they will need to remain calm around the new dog and speak quietly. You may want them to sit or stand still and allow your new Greyhound to approach them first, rather than the other way around. Letting the dog smell the kids before they try to touch him will help the Greyhound understand that the children are not a threat. If you're bringing home a puppy, consider having your chil-dren sit on the floor. This way, they aren't towering over the puppy and won't feel tempted to pick the puppy up, which can lead to serious injuries from dropping.

Depending on the age of your children, you may want to consider assign-ing them chores such as feeding, walking, or cleaning up after the new dog. For many children, caring for an animal can be empowering, so you should consider letting them help when they are able. However, supervision may be necessary, especially for particularly young children.

The Importance of Mutual Respect

When bringing a new animal into your home, it's important to consider the implications of this decision. It can be stressful to bring a Greyhound, or any animal, into your home, and it's crucial for everyone to maintain a certain level of mutual respect. Of course, there will be bumps in the road to happiness, but it's important to make sure both humans and animals are as comfortable as possible. This is especially important if you have kids or other pets in your home. Both children and dogs can easily become over-stimulated while playing and may act inappropriately, which could put both parties in danger. As the adult in the situation, it's your job to monitor any interactions between your existing family members and the new Greyhound.

If your Greyhound seems overwhelmed at any time, it's important to give him a space that he can retreat to and relax. Whether this is a crate or a designated area, he should be able to take a time out periodically. While it's important to respect your new dog's boundaries, you shouldn't forget about your existing pets. Many pets, especially those that have been an only pet for a long time, may not be particularly welcoming toward a new addition. By giving your Greyhound a space of his own to retreat to, you're allowing your other pets a break from any stressful interactions. This designated space will also keep your new dog out of your kids' belongings, which will help eliminate the frustration caused by a puppy chewing up their favorite toy. Though it is incredibly exciting to bring a Greyhound into your home, it can be stressful, so it's important to take precautions to make sure everyone's boundaries are respected during this time.

Preparing Your Other Pets

Before you bring your Greyhound home for the first time, you'll need to consider how you plan on introducing him to your current pets. If you're adopting a Greyhound from a rescue organization, this introduction may even be a necessary step in the adoption process, so it's important to get it right. If your current dogs have dominant personalities, it's important to be cautious during the introduction. Try introducing the dogs on neutral territory outside your home. If you're adopting a Greyhound, this might be at the dog's foster home or a nearby park. If you're bringing home a Greyhound from a breeder, you'll need to find a safe, quiet location for the introduction.

Some Greyhounds will have a higher prey drive than others, so if your current pets are small dogs, cats, or pocket pets, you'll need to be extra cautious during introductions. If the smaller animal gets scared and panics, it could trigger the Greyhound's prey drive, so be sure to safely restrain each animal if possible. If your new Greyhound hasn't encountered small dogs or cats before, he may just need a bit of guidance on appropriate behavior. However, you may need to accept the fact that your new Greyhound won't ever be able to be trusted around your pet rabbit. In many cases, it's perfectly fine to own two different types of animals that never interact. This can be more difficult with small dogs and cats, though, so training may be required before you can allow them to interact off-leash. Always supervise any interactions between your new Greyhound and your current pets until you're completely certain they can be trusted together.

Unique Needs of Rescued Greyhounds

If you've chosen to adopt a Greyhound rather than buy one from a breeder, there are a few things you should know about before you bring your new dog home for the first time. The main challenge you're likely to encounter in your first few weeks at home with your Greyhound is separation anxiety. This is especially true if you don't have other pets in your home. Racing Greyhounds are used to being surrounded by dozens of other dogs in their kennels, with an established routine and familiar handlers. Though many rescued Greyhounds spend some time in a foster home prior to adoption, life in a house away from the track is a new experience, so you'll need to be patient.

It's also important to realize that many rescued Greyhounds aren't yet potty trained in terms of a house. They will be kennel trained and know not to soil their crate, but you'll need frequent potty breaks during the first few weeks and months with your new family member. Remember, rescued

Greyhounds love routine, so if you can establish a regular bathroom break schedule, house training is likely to go much smoother.

These subjects will be discussed more in detail in later chapters, but they are important factors to consider prior to bringing your new Greyhound home for the first time. This way, you'll be able to figure out a bathroom break schedule for your new dog that will work with every family member's existing schedule. You'll also be able to make arrangements for a dog walker if necessary. Knowing that your Greyhound will be a little nervous about being left home alone may also help you plan out the first few days and weeks with your new dog.

Family Commitment

Remember, welcoming a Greyhound into your family is a huge commitment, so before you sign the contract, you need to make sure everyone in your family is in agreement. If one or more members of your family disagree, you may need to reconsider your decision. However, even if all of your family agrees with bringing a Greyhound home, you need to make sure each person knows his or her role in the dog's care.

Photo Courtesy of Arin Wall

Have a family meeting to make sure everyone is on the same page. Not only should you make sure everyone agrees to bring a dog into the family, but you should make sure everyone wants a Greyhound. Have each family member describe their ideal dog, so you know what type of personality your family would like. This will help everyone feel like they're involved in the decision. Making sure your entire family is committed to your new Greyhound's care will make his arrival go much more smoothly.

CHAPTER 6

Preparing Your Home for Your New Greyhound

Creating a Safe Area Indoors

Before bringing your new Greyhound home for the first time, you need to create a safe and comfortable area to help ease him into his new life. If you have other pets in your home, it's likely that your home is already dog-proofed, but new dogs may be able to get into things your existing pets do not, so it's important to make sure your new Greyhound's indoor space is free from danger. The space you set up will also provide your new family member with a place of his own to retreat to should he feel overwhelmed or uncomfortable or if you're unable to supervise him.

Photo Courtesy of Kristy Morris

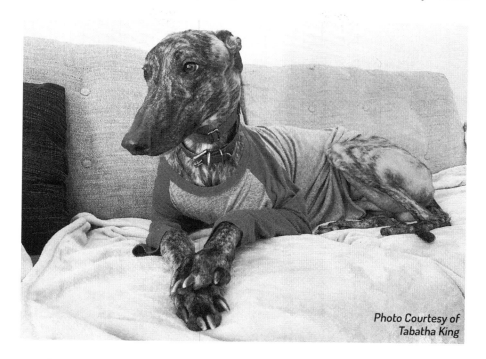

Photo Courtesy of Tabatha King

If you have a small home, it can be difficult to decide what area to temporarily give up to your new Greyhound. Many owners choose their laundry room or a small guest bathroom. You can also section off an area of your kitchen or mudroom. Smaller areas work best, as do areas with easy-to-clean flooring like tile or laminate. If your new Greyhound is still a puppy, you're likely to have more than a few messes to clean up, so it's best to avoid carpeted rooms if possible. Try to choose an area that's out of the way but not isolated. You want to give your Greyhound a quiet space to retreat to, but you don't want him to feel separated from your family.

The most important factor you need to consider when choosing an area is security. Rescued Greyhounds, in particular, can be prone to separation anxiety, and you don't want your new dog to hurt himself trying to escape the first time you leave him alone. If you're using barriers such as baby gates to keep your dog contained, be sure that they are tall enough that the dog can't jump over them. They also need to be attached securely enough so that your Greyhound won't be able to push the barrier over. Playpens are a great option for puppies, but they are generally too flimsy for use with adult dogs. Crates are also an excellent option for any Greyhound. Most rescued Greyhounds have already been crate trained, so they may view the crate as a safe haven that they can retreat to.

Supplies

It's important to make sure you have everything you need before welcoming your new Greyhound into your home. This way, you aren't panicking because you've forgotten to buy food for your new dog. If you have other dogs, you probably have most of what you need already, but it's still helpful to make a list and double-check. If you're worried about your existing pets being unwilling to share their things, you may want to buy extras to make sure there's enough to go around and prevent any resource guarding.

Photo Courtesy of
Hayley Lewis

Here are a few of the basic items that you need for your new Greyhound:

FOOD – Before you bring your new family member home, you'll need to ask the breeder or foster home what type of food they're feeding. Even if this isn't the food you'd like to feed your Greyhound, you'll need to have a small supply of it to help transition him to the food of your choice. If the dog has any food sensitivities, you'll also need to know about this prior to bringing him home.

DOG BED – Greyhounds love to sleep, so you'll need to make sure your new companion is comfortable. If you're bringing home a puppy, it may be helpful to buy an inexpensive bed at first, just in case he decides to chew it up at some point. You can always invest in a higher-quality bed later. Many owners recommend memory foam beds as they can help support large dogs such as Greyhounds. Comfort is especially important for older Greyhounds, so be sure that the bed is thick enough to keep your new dog off the cold floor.

COLLAR AND LEASH – These items are essential as you'll need them right away to take your Greyhound outside for bathroom breaks. The type of collar you choose is up to you, but many Greyhound owners recommend using martingale collars instead of flat buckle collars. The reason for this is that it's very easy for a collar to slide off a Greyhound's slender head. Martingale collars tighten when tension is placed on the leash, but only to a certain point. This prevents the collar from slipping off but won't choke the dog. Many sighthound owners also opt for wider collars as they help disperse the pressure and prevent rubbing. While you're shopping for a new collar and leash, you should also invest in an ID tag with your contact information to help reunite you with your new Greyhound should he escape.

GROOMING SUPPLIES – Even if you plan on taking your Greyhound to a professional groomer, you'll probably want a few grooming supplies on hand just in case. Besides, the more practice your dog gets with grooming and handling, the better he'll behave for a professional. A soft bristle brush or rubber curry brush can help remove dead hair and stimulate blood flow to the skin. You might also want to have shampoo, conditioner, or grooming wipes on hand just in case your Greyhound gets dirty between grooming appointments. If you want to trim your dog's nails yourself, you'll need to buy a high-quality nail clipper or grinder. If you're unsure of what types of grooming supplies are best for a Greyhound, be sure to ask your local groomer for advice. Grooming supplies will also be discussed in a later chapter.

HOUSETRAINING SUPPLIES – Whether you're bringing home a puppy or an adult Greyhound, it's a good idea to have some housetraining supplies available. Even a dog that has been properly housetrained can have a few accidents because of the stress of moving into a new home. Many rescued Greyhounds know not to relieve themselves in their crate, but they may not understand that the rule applies to the rest of the house too. Be sure to purchase a cleaning product designed for pet messes, as they often have enzymes to help eliminate odor and staining. You might also consider buying disposable or reusable puppy pads. Crate training is also an important part of the housetraining process, so be sure to purchase an appropriately sized crate for your Greyhound.

Basic Shopping List for Your New Greyhound

- Collar and leash
- Identification tag
- Crate
- Bedding
- Food
- Treats
- Toys
- Combs or brushes
- Shampoo
- Nail trimmer
- Puppy pads
- Cleaning supplies

Photo Courtesy of
Birgit Neumann

Dog-Proofing Your House

Once you've acquired the necessary supplies to make your Greyhound comfortable in his new home, it's time to ensure your home is safe for him. If you have other dogs, your home is likely pretty safe already, but it doesn't hurt to go through once or twice more to make sure there's nothing that could hurt a dog that's new to that environment. The best way to accomplish this is to go through your home room by room. Getting down on your Greyhound's level will help you spot any potential dangers. Of course, you shouldn't leave your Greyhound unsupervised outside of his crate or area during the first few weeks or even months, but you should still make sure there's nothing that he could potentially ingest or be injured by.

HELPFUL TIP
Buying a Crate

When buying supplies for your new Greyhound, it's important not to skip the crate. Even if you don't intend to utilize a crate as a training tool, providing a crate can be a sanctuary for your new dog. If a crate isn't part of your long-term training regimen, consider a foldable crate that can be folded and stored flat. Since Greyhounds are not only large dogs but also tall, be sure to choose a crate that will be comfortable for your dog to lie down in, as well as stand up and turn around. If you're adopting a puppy and want to choose a crate that your dog can grow into, purchase a crate with a removable divider. Putting your puppy in a crate that's too large can derail your house-training efforts.

In rooms such as the kitchen and bathroom, you might consider installing childproof locks for the cabinets, especially if they contain harmful products such as cleaning supplies or trash cans. You'll also want to remove any houseplants from your new dog's reach, even if they are non-toxic to pets. This will help prevent damage to your plants as well as eliminating the need to clean up the mess of a broken pot and soil everywhere. Don't forget about floor-length window coverings while you're Greyhound proofing your home.

Be sure to pick up all electrical cords or remove those items from your Greyhound's reach. Picking up cords is especially important if you're bringing home a puppy or a former racing Greyhound that will be unfamiliar with these items and may try to chew on them. Plastic zip ties are a great way to organize electrical cords and keep them out of any dog's reach. Plus, they're easy to remove once you feel confident that your Greyhound will leave the cords alone.

You'll want to remove any temptations that might be lying around on the floor. Clothing, shoes, and children's toys should all be stored safely out of the dog's reach. A curious Greyhound could easily swallow a small toy or item of clothing in an instant.

Indoor Dangers

As previously stated, electrical cords are a common indoor danger present in most rooms of the house. Puppies tend to explore their environment using their mouths, so an electrical cord might seem like a fun new chew toy for a curious young Greyhound, especially if he's teething. While an electrical shock is unlikely to be fatal, it could seriously burn your dog's mouth.

Another common indoor danger is household chemicals such as cleaning products and pesticides. This also includes medication and any beauty or hygiene products you might have in your cabinets. If you're a houseplant enthusiast, you'll also need to keep your pest control products and fertilizers out of your Greyhound's reach.

It's also crucial to make sure that your houseplants themselves don't present any danger to your new dog. Many types of houseplants are non-toxic if ingested, but there are quite a few that could cause problems. Those problems could range from mild gastrointestinal upset to seizures or death, so it's important to know what types of plants you have in your home. The ASPCA has a list of common houseplants and their toxicity on their website that you can consult if you're unsure.

If your home has stairs, you may also want to consider keeping your new Greyhound away from them, especially if you're bringing home a puppy or senior. Safely moving up or down stairs requires a fair amount of strength and agility, which most young and old dogs lack. Consider installing pressure-mounted baby gates to keep your Greyhound safe and eliminate the worry of falling.

As you search through your house for potential dangers, don't forget about your trash cans. Trash cans can be incredibly hazardous as they can contain anything from food scraps and leftovers to broken objects and packaging. Once your Greyhound learns that the trash can contains something tasty, you're going to have a difficult time getting him to leave it alone. This bad habit is self-rewarding and can be incredibly difficult to break. Plus, every time your dog gets into the trash, he's at risk of consuming something dangerous. Prevention is the best option, so consider investing in a locking trash can if you can't hide it in a cabinet or closet.

Outdoor Dangers

After you've checked your home for potential dangers, it's time to move outside. One of the most common outdoor dangers is a damaged fence. Loose boards, holes, rotten wood, or even damaged latches can allow a clever Greyhound to escape. This could potentially put him at risk of getting hit by a car, being stolen, or getting into trouble with wildlife or a stray dog. Additionally, short fences are quite easy for an adult Greyhound to leap over, so you need to make sure your yard is secure.

If you have a pool, you'll also need to make sure that area is secure. Pool fencing is the easiest way to keep your Greyhound out, but you need to make sure the gaps between the rails are small enough that your Greyhound, especially if he's a puppy, won't be able to squeeze through. If your pool is unfenced, you'll need to make sure your dog never has unsupervised access to it. Accidents can happen in the blink of an eye, and a panicked dog may not be able to find his way out of the water.

Just as you did indoors, you'll need to make sure your yard or garden doesn't contain any plants that could be toxic to your Greyhound should he eat them. If you do have toxic plants, fence them off or remove them. Fencing off your garden is also a great way to prevent your Greyhound from digging or relieving himself in it.

Finally, you'll need to make sure your Greyhound can't get into your garage or shed, as those types of buildings often contain harmful items such as pesticides, rat poison, and antifreeze. Antifreeze, in particular, poses a danger to any animal. It has a sweet, appealing flavor, so most animals are eager to lap it up when they find it. Unfortunately, it causes permanent kidney damage or even death, so be sure to clean up any spills and make sure your garage or shed can't be accessed by your new dog.

Crates and Crate Training

Whether you're getting your new Greyhound from a breeder or from a rescue organization, the crate can be an excellent training tool. Even if you plan on eventually phasing out the crate, it's still an important part of any dog's education. If your Greyhound ever needs to be kenneled at the vet or groomer, he'll be able to patiently wait his turn without panicking or injuring himself or others.

Dogs that lack proper crate training view the crate as a punishment rather than a source of comfort. They usually have to be forced into the crate and may panic once inside. Not only does this make the dog difficult for professionals such as veterinary staff to handle, but the dog could become seriously injured. Greyhounds are notorious for having thin skin, and they can cause serious lacerations trying to escape their crate. Broken nails and teeth are common injuries. Dogs without crate training may also bark incessantly or relieve themselves in the crate. This is why it's important to set your Greyhound up for success and teach him that crates are resting places that shouldn't be feared.

Before you begin crate training, you'll need to decide what type of crate you want to use. Crates are available in a wide range of materials, including wood, plastic, and metal. Metal wire crates are the most popular type as they are relatively sturdy and inexpensive. However, they rarely stand up to dogs intent on breaking out. Wood crates are typically the most expensive and aesthetically pleasing, but they, too, rarely stand up to destructive dogs. Plastic crates are also a common choice. They're usually budget-friendly, airline-approved, and some are even crash-test rated. If you're worried about your Greyhound trying to escape, it's best to look for high-anxiety or heavy-duty metal crates. These types are designed to stand up to even the most determined dogs, but they aren't cheap. For Greyhounds that are already crate trained, you should be able to choose any type without worrying about your dog hurting himself.

It's also important to choose the right size crate for your Greyhound. Greyhounds are large dogs, so you'll need to look for a relatively large kennel. Ideally, your dog should have enough room to comfortably stand up, turn around, and lie down. Bigger is not always better, however, as you don't want to give him enough room to encourage him to relieve himself inside. If you're bringing home a Greyhound puppy, you might want to use inexpensive wire or plastic crates as you'll likely need to upgrade as he grows. Some crates have removable dividers that can adjust the size of the accessible space in the crate.

To begin crate training your Greyhound, you want to make the space as comfortable and appealing as possible. If you're sure he won't chew anything up, you can put a bed, blankets, and even his favorite toy inside. If you're putting things in the crate without certainty that your new dog won't destroy them, it's best to supervise him until you're sure. Otherwise, he could chew things up and swallow them, putting him at risk of choking or an intestinal blockage.

Next, you want to encourage your new Greyhound to go inside his new crate. Start by tossing a few treats inside and letting him go in without shutting the door. At first, he'll probably grab the treats and go right back out, but with plenty of praise and treats, he'll start spending more time inside. At that point, you can try shutting the door for just a moment. Be sure to reward him for quiet behavior while inside. As the dog becomes more comfortable, you can leave him inside for longer periods of time.

The most important factor of proper crate training is to not let your Greyhound out if he's whining or barking. This just reinforces bad behavior and rewards him for complaining. He'll quickly learn that the fastest way out of the crate is to throw a fit about it. Instead, give him a few minutes to get over it and calmly release him when he's quiet.

Greyhounds and Extreme Temperatures

Greyhounds tend to be quite sensitive to extreme temperatures, whether cold or hot. Remember, these dogs have very little body fat and a thin coat, so they lack the insulation that many other breeds possess. This means you'll need to be particularly conscientious about your dog's exposure to extreme temperatures during the summer and winter. This is not a breed that can live comfortably outdoors in most climates.

During the summer, you'll need to make sure that your Greyhound has access to clean, fresh water at all times. Hydration is key in temperature control. Most Greyhounds have few problems tolerating even the hottest summers as long as they have water and an air-conditioned room or house to retreat to. Never leave your Greyhound unattended outside for long periods of time when it's hot out, especially if it's humid too.

During the winter, you should take extra precautions to protect your Greyhound from the cold. Consider purchasing a sweater or jacket to make up for his lack of fur and body fat. Most Greyhounds adapt quickly to wearing clothing. Since Greyhounds have a somewhat unique body shape, look for jackets designed specifically for sighthounds to ensure the best fit. You might also consider investing in booties if your Greyhound has sensitive feet. Booties will help protect paws against the damaging effects of salt on the sidewalks or roads where you walk. It might seem excessive to bundle your Greyhound up for a quick bathroom break, but your dog's comfort should always be your priority.

CHAPTER 7
Bringing Your New Greyhound Home

The Importance of Having a Plan

Bringing any new dog into your home is going to be stressful, but with proper planning, your first few days with your new Greyhound will be as stress-free as possible. One of the most important and often overlooked

Photo Courtesy of Karen Robertson

aspects of welcoming a new member of the family is deciding on household rules. Before your Greyhound comes home for the first time, consider sitting down with your family and deciding what boundaries you want your new dog to have. Will you be allowing him on the furniture? Will he be eating or sleeping in a certain spot in the house? By discussing these rules ahead of time, you'll be able to make sure that everyone can enforce the rules consistently once your Greyhound arrives.

Photo Courtesy of Amy King

You might also want to consider writing down not only the rules of the house but everyone's roles in the new Greyhound's care. This is particularly helpful with young or forgetful members of the family who need a visual representation of their responsibilities. Decide who is in charge of walking, feeding, training, etc. Consistency is the fastest way to help your Greyhound settle in.

Picking Your Greyhound Up from the Breeder

As long as you've been thorough in your preparations, picking up your Greyhound from the breeder shouldn't be a big deal. However, it's worth double-checking everything the day before you're scheduled to pick up your new dog to make sure you have everything you need. It's important to eliminate the need for any last-minute stops at the pet store. Not only will this make the ride home more stressful for your new puppy, but a minimally vaccinated puppy could be at risk of picking up dangerous viruses by visiting public places before being fully vaccinated.

If your breeder requires you to sign a contract, you may have already done so prior to picking up your new Greyhound, but if you haven't, take one last moment to read through the document and make sure the information contained in it is accurate and that you agree to all clauses. That contract is legally binding, so it's essential that you know what you're agreeing to. If you've only paid a deposit and not the full purchase price, you'll also want to be sure to get cash or a check ready to hand over to the breeder at pickup.

Before you leave to pick up your Greyhound, you might also want to think of any questions you may still have about your new puppy or about Greyhounds in general. Reputable breeders are happy to stay in touch after you bring your dog home, so don't worry if you can't think of any questions or forget to ask at pickup.

Bringing Your Greyhound Home from the Rescue

Just as with bringing a Greyhound home from a breeder, if you've done the proper preparations, welcoming home your rescued Greyhound should be a low-key event. Again, you'll want to make sure that if you have any questions about your dog or the breed in general, you write them down so that you can ask rescue staff or volunteers before you take your Greyhound home. Most reputable rescues will be available if you have questions later. You'll also want to make sure that the adoption paperwork has been read through and that you agree to everything contained within it. Finally, don't forget the cash or check to cover the adoption fee.

Photo Courtesy of
Susan Berthold

The Ride Home

Though many dog owners put little thought into the ride home from the breeder or rescue, this is a crucial part of the process. Unless your Greyhound is an experienced traveler, it's impossible to predict how he'll behave in the car, so it's best to assume that he's going to be nervous.

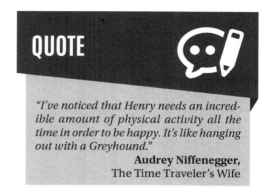

QUOTE

"I've noticed that Henry needs an incredible amount of physical activity all the time in order to be happy. It's like hanging out with a Greyhound."

Audrey Niffenegger,
The Time Traveler's Wife

Safety should always be your priority when traveling with your Greyhound, so be sure you have some sort of restraint available. It can be tempting to ride home with your new Greyhound puppy in your lap or your adult Greyhound loose in the back seat, but these choices can be dangerous if you get into a wreck. There are many different types of restraints that work for a range of dogs, so you may need to line up one method for the ride home and try out any others at a later time.

Most dogs, especially rescued Greyhounds, are comfortable traveling in a crate. The only challenge is finding a crate large enough to comfortably house your Greyhound in the car. If you have a small vehicle, you may need to consider other options, but most SUVs are large enough to handle a large crate. You might also consider asking the breeder or foster home for a blanket or toy with a familiar scent on it to help ease your Greyhound's anxiety.

Doggie seatbelts are another great option. Most seatbelts designed for dogs are able to either connect to your car's existing seat belts or wrap around the headrests. The other end of the lead attaches to your dog's harness. When choosing a harness for the car, it's best to go with harnesses with wide chest plates to help spread out the pressure should you have to brake suddenly or get into an accident.

Barriers, made from either fabric or metal, are also great options. These products usually install just behind the driver and passenger seats, or they may separate the cargo area from the seats in front of it. No matter which option works best for you and your vehicle, prioritizing the safety of your Greyhound and your family is crucial.

Motion sickness is a possibility with any dog, especially a nervous traveler, so you may want to consider bringing along extra towels, blankets, or puppy pads. Disposable or reusable puppy pads are a great way to line a kennel to make cleanup a breeze. If you are using a barrier or seatbelt, consider using a waterproof seat cover or cargo area cover to help keep your vehicle mess-free.

You also need to remember that no matter how your Greyhound reacts in the car, you need to stay calm. Some dogs may react by shaking nervously, while others may panic and try to escape. This is also why restraints are so important, as you don't want to be driving down the freeway in heavy traffic when your new dog decides he doesn't want to be in the car anymore. However, proper restraints combined with a calm and collected attitude will help your dog understand that there is nothing to be afraid of.

The First Night Home

If you have a choice on when to bring your new Greyhound home, it's best to do so on a day where you don't have any early morning appointments the next day. It's likely that your new Greyhound will be stressed about moving out of a familiar environment into a new home, so your night could be sleepless. Regardless of the age of your new Greyhound, he may be quite restless or upset during the first night, so it's important to be patient and not stress about getting sleep.

If you've done your planning before bringing your Greyhound home, you've likely already decided where he will be sleeping. While it may be tempting to put a whining puppy out of earshot, the isolation will likely upset him further. Instead, it's best to put a crate or playpen in your bedroom near your bed. This way, your new dog won't be alone. This is recommended over allowing him free rein of your bedroom. A nervous and possibly unhouse-trained dog is almost guaranteed to make a mess if you give him access to the entire room or house the first night.

The first night home with your Greyhound will set the stage for your new nightly routine, so be sure to take him out as late as possible before you go to bed. If you've brought home a puppy, you're going to be getting up several times a night to let him out, so by taking him out just before bedtime, you will hopefully be able to get a few hours of sleep in before the next bathroom break. The general rule of thumb for this is that your puppy can go an average of one hour for every month of his age before needing a break. So, if you've brought home a puppy that is eight weeks old, or two months, you should plan on taking him out every two hours. An adult Greyhound should technically be able to hold it all night, but you might consider taking him

49

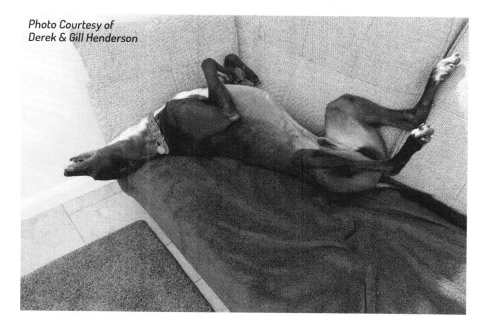

Photo Courtesy of
Derek & Gill Henderson

out at least once during the night to ensure that he doesn't make a mess, especially if you aren't sure of his housetraining status.

You should also be aware that your new Greyhound may whine or cry during his first night, especially if he's a puppy who is spending his first night away from his mother and littermates. You'll need to determine whether those cries mean he's ready for a bathroom break or if he's just lonely. If he's recently gone outside, you can be certain that it's probably just a tantrum. Unless it's been a few hours and your Greyhound needs a bathroom break, ignore his cries. Giving him affection to comfort him will only encourage this type of behavior, so you need to wait for him to settle down before paying attention to him. It's also helpful to take note of how often your Greyhound needs to go out during the night so you can establish a regular nightly routine.

CHAPTER 8
The First Few Weeks

Standing by Your Expectations

It's almost guaranteed that during the first few weeks with your new Greyhound, you're going to encounter a few challenges. However, it's important to keep your expectations reasonable to avoid being disappointed by your new dog. Remember, this is a big change for your dog too. It can take several weeks or even months for a dog to adapt to life in a new household. If you spend a half-hour every week working on your Greyhound's manners, you're not going to see the same results as you would if you spent just 10 minutes every day training him. Infrequent training and inconsistency will cause both you and your dog to become frustrated.

FUN FACT
Greyhound Bus

Today, the Greyhound bus is a ubiquitous symbol of mass transit. Founded by a Swedish immigrant named Carl Wickman, who began providing transportation to miners in Minnesota, the ensuing company didn't adopt the name Greyhound until 1929. The story goes that a bus operator named Ed Stone was driving his bus route from Superior to Wausau, Wisconsin, and saw the reflection of his bus in a store window. The reflection reminded him of a Greyhound dog, and he decided to name his route after the Greyhound. Eventually the name became so popular that it was adopted as the company name.

This is not to say that you should spend every waking moment training your Greyhound. It's important to establish the rules up front, but you need to be patient during the first few weeks. This is a stressful time in your dog's life, and he likely won't be completely interested in listening to every command you give him. Instead, start small and keep things simple until your Greyhound is ready to progress further. Even if he doesn't learn any real commands but makes small progress in his housetraining or staying home alone, you can consider it a win.

Photo Courtesy of
Clair Cuthbertson

Establishing Household Rules

During the first few weeks at home with your Greyhound, you'll need to introduce him to the rules of the house. Since you'll have already discussed these boundaries with the other human members of your family, you'll need to work together to make sure your new dog understands. Each person will need to be involved in order to achieve the consistency it takes to teach a dog how to behave in the house.

One of the most important rules for any dog to know is that they are not allowed to go through doorways before humans. It's incredibly rude for a dog to shove his way through the door first, and Greyhounds are big enough that they could easily knock over and injure a small child or older person. Additionally, your dog's own safety is at risk if he manages to shove his way out the front door and runs off. Introduce this rule by having your Greyhound sit or stand quietly each and every time you open a door. During the first few times you introduce this concept, he's likely to get excited and attempt to rush through the door. If he attempts to go through before you allow it, return him to the sitting or standing position in which he started. Once he's waiting patiently, then you can allow him to go through the door after you. You can also use a release word such as "OK" if you'd like.

Another important household rule is moving out of the way when asked. As the one in charge, you get to choose where you sit, stand, or lie down, and your dog must move out of your way when you ask him. Whether you're asking him to step out of the kitchen while you prepare a meal or asking him to get off the bed so you can get in, it's important for him to move right away.

Allowing your dog to stay where he is so that you have to move around him will convince him that he's in charge.

Most Greyhounds have few problems with this concept once they understand it, but there are a few different ways to introduce this idea. The first method is to have your dog wear a "drag line," which is simply a short leash designed to be dragged around the house so you can grab it and correct the dog when necessary. They're typically long enough to grab safely without being so long that they get tangled up on furniture or other household objects. If your Greyhound is highly motivated by food, you can also lure him out of the way while giving him an appropriate verbal command such as "off" or "move." You can also use it to pull your dog out of the way with his collar or push him out of the way, but you need to use caution with these methods until you know your Greyhound better. Some dogs don't respond well to this pressure and may snap. Most owners find success using a combination of using the drag line and luring with treats for positive reinforcement.

Photo Courtesy of
Susie Morris

Puppy Problems

If you're bringing home a Greyhound puppy, you're going to experience some challenges that you wouldn't face if you adopted an adult dog. However, as long as you correct your puppy's behavior consistently and make your expectations clear, you should be able to easily prevent bad habits from developing. With puppies, supervision is key. Many bad behaviors are self-rewarding, so you need to supervise well enough that your puppy never has the chance to engage in such behaviors.

One of the most common challenges faced by Greyhound puppy owners is chewing. Chewing is not unique to Greyhounds, as all breeds go through this phase while teething. Though most puppies chew some during their first few months of life, it's usually nothing more than a method of helping them explore their surroundings. However, between the ages of four and six months, their puppy teeth will be replaced with adult teeth in a frustrating and sometimes painful process. Most puppies begin chewing during this time to help them cope with the discomfort of teething. During this time, you need to supervise your puppy and provide him with plenty of safe chews or toys so that he doesn't have the opportunity to chew on inappropriate items like furniture and shoes.

Greyhounds are not as prone to digging as other breeds, such as terriers, but they can still develop this bad habit if given the chance. Allowing your Greyhound puppy to wander around your outdoor space unsupervised is asking for trouble. Once he begins this behavior and doesn't receive correction, he'll begin to do it more and more. Then when you do correct him, he'll become confused as he's always been allowed to act like this before. Note that digging is not only an outdoor problem. Many puppies dig at furniture or potted plants while indoors. Digging is a messy habit, but it's also potentially dangerous as your dog can damage his nails and paw pads or ingest rocks, sticks, or soil. Plus, digging may allow your Greyhound puppy to escape your yard. To prevent any injuries or damages to your home associated with digging, be sure to supervise your puppy any time he's out of his crate and correct any naughty behavior immediately.

Most Greyhounds are relatively quiet dogs, but excessive barking can be a frustrating habit that some puppies develop. Most of the time, a bark or two to alert you to something isn't a problem, but any more than that can become a problem. Excessive barking is a common behavior associated with separation anxiety and a lack of physical and mental stimulation. Again, supervision and consistent behavior correction are key.

To correct your Greyhound puppy's bad behaviors, most of the time, a loud clap or stomp or a sharp "No!" should be enough to stop him in his tracks. With repetition, your Greyhound will understand that this unpleasant noise is associated with a certain behavior, and he'll stop barking or digging. Greyhounds are usually quite sensitive, but some individuals may be more resistant to correction than others. If you need a stronger correction, consider using a spray bottle filled with water in combination with a verbal reprimand. Spraying your dog in the face with water won't hurt him, but it's unpleasant enough to let him know you don't approve of his actions. No matter what, never hit, kick, or scream at your Greyhound as a correction. He will not understand that you're correcting him and may react fearfully. Greyhounds are sensitive dogs that react badly to strong corrections, so it's best to use as light of a touch as possible.

Rescued Dog Problems

One of the most common problems faced by owners of rescued Greyhounds is separation anxiety. Greyhounds that have been used for racing are usually quite fond of people and are constantly around other Greyhounds, so the first time they are left alone in their new home can be frightening.

In order to minimize the stress associated with leaving your dog home alone, don't make a big deal out of leaving the house or entering it. Your dog might get excited, but you need to ignore him until he's calmed down. It might be a struggle to resist that drawn-out goodbye or excited hello, but quietly exit your house without getting your dog too riled up. When you get your Greyhound excited about your departure or arrival, you're just enforcing his belief that there's something to be concerned about. However, if you don't acknowledge him until he's calm, he'll begin to understand that there's no reason to worry, and you'll be back soon.

You can introduce this concept by putting your shoes on, grabbing your keys, and heading out the door. Stay outside for just a moment before coming back inside and putting everything away. Ignore your dog's excitement and repeat the process. The more you repeat the actions of leaving the house and returning without paying attention to your dog, the less interested he's going to be when you leave for real.

Leaving Your Dog Home Alone

The first few times you leave your Greyhound home alone will be stressful for you both. The key is to remain calm and confident. If you seem stressed about leaving your dog, he's going to worry too. As previously stated, the more you can practice leaving the house without making a big deal out of it,

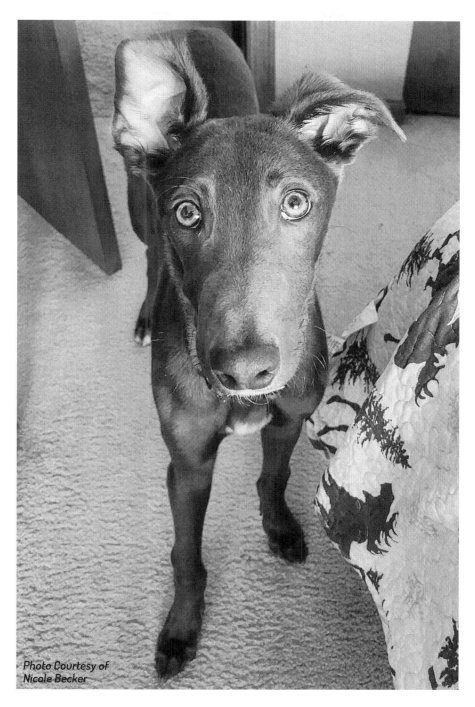

Photo Courtesy of Nicole Becker

the better your dog is going to be when you do actually need to go to work or run errands.

Crate training is incredibly helpful for dogs with separation anxiety. While it might seem counterintuitive to lock a nervous dog up in a crate while you're gone, most dogs learn to see the crate as a source of comfort, like a den.

If your Greyhound seems particularly concerned about being left home alone, you may also want to consider getting him a companion. Rescued Greyhounds, in particular, have lived their entire lives in groups and tend to gain comfort from the presence of other Greyhounds. A companion might be just what he needs to rest comfortably until you return. The companion doesn't necessarily need to be a Greyhound. A dog of another breed or even a cat may be fine. However, since some Greyhounds can have high prey drives, it's important to know how your Greyhound will respond to a small dog or cat before bringing one into your home.

Training Classes

During the first few weeks with your Greyhound, you may want to look for local training classes to give you a boost in teaching your Greyhound the basics. Though most Greyhounds will never be obedience ring stars, training classes are a great way to build a bond with your new dog and exercise his mind while also socializing him to new experiences. In a basic training class, the dog will learn simple commands such as sit, down, and stay, which will help you enforce the rules of your household and have the best relationship possible with your new companion.

For puppy classes, dogs must typically be under six months of age, though some puppy classes may go up to a year. Participants will need to be at least 16 weeks of age so that they are fully vaccinated. It's recommended to wait until your puppy has received all of his shots before taking him to a training class as disease and parasites can spread quickly. Most training facilities will require proof of vaccination and possibly also flea and tick prevention before you are allowed to come to class.

If you've adopted an adult Greyhound, puppy classes won't be an option. However, most training facilities also offer beginning obedience classes targeting adult dogs of any age. You may be able to find these classes at a formal training facility, individual trainer, or even shelter or dog sport club. Classes may be offered in public areas, or you can have a trainer give you private lessons in your home or at a nearby park. If your Greyhound has any behavioral issues, you may want to seek one-on-one lessons before attending any group classes.

Take It Slow

The most important aspect of spending the first few weeks with your new Greyhound is patience and understanding. You're guaranteed to hit a few bumps in the road as you get to know each other, but it's important to be patient no matter how challenging your troubles may seem. Welcoming a Greyhound into your home isn't easy, but with time it will be one of the most rewarding experiences of your life.

As mentioned earlier in the chapter, it's crucial to keep your expectations low during this adjustment period. Your Greyhound is experiencing a lot of new and scary things, and you need to understand that he may not be in the right place mentally to tackle training as well. Keep your training sessions short and sweet, with plenty of positive reinforcement. If you get stuck on a certain task, try going back to something your dog already knows just so you can reward him for something. Then you can return to the difficult task in a later session. This will help prevent frustration and resentment from building, and you'll both look forward to the next training session with each other.

CHAPTER 9
Health and Wellness

Choosing a Veterinarian

Unless your new Greyhound is your first pet, you may already have a preferred veterinarian. If you don't, you'll need to perform a bit of research to ensure you choose a reputable veterinary clinic to take your Greyhound to for both preventative and emergency care. In some cases, you may need to work with two clinics if your preferred clinic has limited hours or does not do emergencies.

HELPFUL TIP
Bloat

Gastric dilatation-volvulus, commonly known as bloat, is a medical emergency and is more likely to occur in dogs with deep, narrow chests such as Greyhounds. Bloat happens when a dog's stomach fills with gas and cuts off the blood supply to a dog's gut. Learning to spot the symptoms of this rare but life-threatening problem can make an impact on your dog's survival. Symptoms can include:
- Swollen belly that's hard to the touch
- Pain in abdomen when touched
- Drooling
- Dry-heaving
- Restlessness

Reference: https://www.ctvsh.com/services/dogs/breeds/Greyhound

If your Greyhound's breeder is local, you may want to ask for a recommendation on a new vet. If the vet is familiar with the breeder's dogs, you'll know that he or she is familiar with common health problems in the breed and has likely seen your new dog since he was a young puppy. If you've rescued your Greyhound from a local rescue organization, they may also be able to recommend a vet in your area.

Unfortunately, if the breeder or rescue you've been working with is in another city or state, they won't be able to help you. Your next resources to consult are dog-loving friends and family, especially if you know anyone with Greyhounds.

If you happen to know any groomers, trainers, or dog sport competitors, they may also be able to recommend a vet that they know and trust.

Prior to beginning your search for a new vet, you might want to consider what type of vet clinic you want to take your Greyhound to for medical care. The vast majority of vet clinics practice traditional veterinary medicine, but there are plenty of holistic vets that also perform alternative therapies. You may also consult the directories available on the websites of the American Holistic Veterinary Medical Association (AHVMA) and American Veterinary Medical Association (AVMA).

As previously mentioned, not all clinics are open 24/7, so you may also need to seek out a local veterinary clinic in case your Greyhound falls ill or becomes injured on a holiday or in the middle of the night. Some clinics may be open during normal business hours and will be on-call during the off-hours, while others are open 24/7. If finances are a concern, you should also look for low-cost vaccination and spaying or neutering clinics.

What to Expect During the First Visit

It's important not to be anxious for your Greyhound's first visit to the vet to help reduce any nervousness your Greyhound may already be experiencing. He'll pick up on your mood, so stay calm. His first visit is likely to be uneventful, so there's no need to worry. During his first trip to the vet, your Greyhound will probably undergo a physical examination in addition to being weighed and having his temperature, pulse, and respirations taken. If he's deemed to be healthy, he will receive any vaccinations, deworming, or testing that he may be due for.

The exact care your Greyhound receives during his first vet visit will depend on his age and health history. If you've brought home a puppy, he'll likely need to return within a few weeks to receive booster vaccinations, whereas an adult Greyhound may not need to come back until his next checkup. If you have your new dog's vaccination history, it's helpful to give it to the vet so that they can send out a reminder when your Greyhound is due for his next vaccine.

It's important to note that in most cases, puppies will not be fully vaccinated until at least 16 weeks of age. This is due to the age requirement for the administration of the rabies vaccine. Until your Greyhound puppy has received all of his vaccines, it's important to limit his exposure to the outside world, even if he's already had one or two shots. Diseases like distemper or parvovirus can be easily contracted by puppies and may be fatal, so it's important to avoid public places and limit the number of new dogs and humans you introduce your young Greyhound to before he's fully vaccinated.

Caring for Sighthounds

In many ways, sighthounds are just like any other dog, but there are a few key differences in their care. The most significant problem to look out for is that many sighthounds, including Greyhounds, have an abnormal

Photo Courtesy of Birgit Neumann

sensitivity to anesthesia. Though some sighthounds do just fine under anesthesia, it's not uncommon for these dogs to have prolonged recovery times with certain anesthetic drugs. The reason these dogs struggle with recovery is a lack of the hepatic enzyme responsible for the metabolism of certain anesthetic drugs. Thiopental and propofol are the most common drugs to cause a delayed recovery in Greyhounds and other sighthounds. Additionally, sighthounds are known for their lean physiques and low body fat, which can present a problem with lipophilic drugs, which are fat-soluble. Many anesthetic drugs are lipophilic, so again, it's important to consult a veterinarian knowledgeable in sighthound care before allowing your Greyhound to undergo any procedure requiring anesthesia.

Additionally, healthy adult Greyhounds sometimes have slightly different bloodwork results than most breeds. They may show a low platelet count or low thyroid reading despite their apparent good health. Other values may also be slightly low or high compared to the average dog, but a veterinarian familiar with sighthounds will be able to accurately interpret the results despite the apparently abnormal readings.

These problems are relatively easy to manage as long as you work with a veterinarian well versed in Greyhound care. Though Greyhounds are a healthy breed, they are prone to a few medical conditions in addition to the unique problems mentioned in this chapter. Common health problems will be discussed in more detail in Chapter 18.

Dangerous Foods

Most dog owners are aware of dangerous foods like chocolate, alcohol, and even caffeine. However, there are plenty of other human foods that are toxic to dogs. Both the AKC and ASPCA websites have lists of common toxic foods on their websites. Some foods are just toxic enough to cause digestive upset, but others can be fatal if your Greyhound consumes them. One of the most dangerous ingredients in many human foods is xylitol, which is a sweetener commonly used in sugar-free foods like candy, chewing gum, and peanut butter. Xylitol can be lethal even if your dog only eats a small amount. Onions and garlic are also dangerous as they contain N-propyl disulfide, which damages red blood cells in dogs. Though the toxic substance in grapes and raisins has yet to be identified, these foods can cause serious kidney problems, including kidney failure. If your Greyhound accidentally eats any of these foods, it's important to seek veterinary treatment immediately. The sooner your dog can be seen by a vet, the more likely he is to survive.

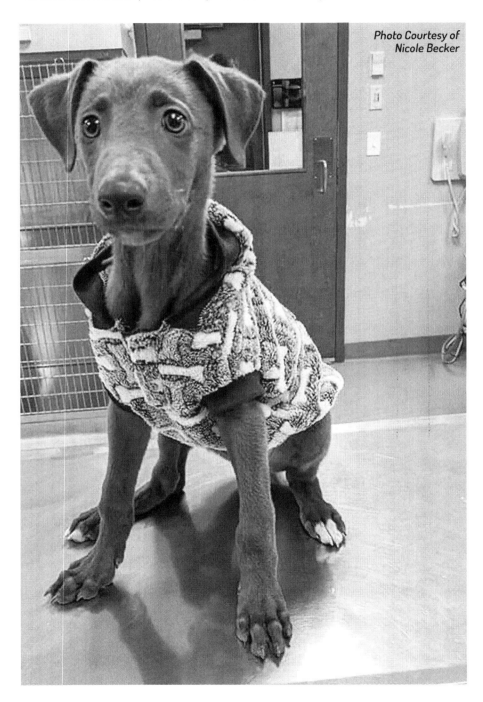

Photo Courtesy of
Nicole Becker

The toxic foods listed here are not the only human foods to be wary of around your Greyhound. There are also plenty of "safe" human foods that should only be fed sparingly to your dog, if at all. High-fat foods like peanut butter and cheese are examples, as the fat content can contribute to obesity and pancreatitis. Salty foods, such as popcorn, ham, and bacon, should also be avoided or fed sparingly. Many dogs can also experience serious digestive upset if they eat too much dairy, such as yogurt and cottage cheese. In addition to lactose, ice cream contains a lot of sugar, so it's not something you should feed your Greyhound in large amounts. Candy and cookies should also be avoided due to their high sugar content.

Common Health Problems in Puppies

One of the most common health problems with puppies is internal parasites. Internal parasites can be easily picked up by any puppy in the womb or through their mother's milk. Contaminated food, water, soil, and feces are also common sources when ingested. The exact type of worms that could affect your Greyhound puppy will vary according to your location but may include roundworms, tapeworms, whipworms, and hookworms. Heartworms are also common, as are protozoa like coccidia and giardia.

Though some puppies may show no obvious symptoms of a parasitic infection, common symptoms include vomiting, diarrhea, anemia, and sudden weight loss. Some puppies may also have a malnourished body and distended stomach. Other symptoms include coughing and lethargy. Since some puppies will not show signs of internal parasites, testing is crucial, especially if you suspect your Greyhound has been exposed to parasites.

Internal parasites are not the only parasites to be worried about, as external parasites are also common in puppies. Ticks and fleas are the most common parasites that can easily be acquired from other pets or outdoor spaces. Dogs that are infested with fleas and ticks may experience hair loss, skin inflammation, and itching. Flea allergy dermatitis can also occur as the dog's immune system reacts to the fleas' saliva. Many puppies with serious parasite loads may also experience lethargy and anemia. Additionally, fleas and ticks commonly carry internal parasites such as tapeworms, as well as diseases like Rocky Mountain spotted fever, Lyme disease, babesiosis, and ehrlichiosis. External parasites may also be passed from animals to humans, putting all members of your family at risk. This is why it's important to treat parasites as soon as possible. Since parasites vary by location, it's best to consult your vet about which fleas and ticks are common in your area and what product is best for prevention or treatment.

Photo Courtesy of Dexter Corcoran

Another common problem with puppies is digestive upset. No matter what type of food you feed your Greyhound, he's bound to eventually get into something that will upset his stomach. It's also possible for stress or sudden changes in diet or lifestyle to cause digestive problems, especially for particularly sensitive dogs. Vomiting and diarrhea are common in these instances but rarely have any long-term effects on your puppy's overall health. Most of the time, symptoms will disappear after a day or two without the need for a vet visit. However, if the symptoms continue beyond just a day or two, or you see blood in your Greyhound's stool or changes in his behavior, contact your veterinarian. These can be signs of a more serious issue, so it's important to see a vet as soon as possible. It's also important that you make any changes in diet slowly, over a period of about seven to ten days. This will help minimize any digestive upset due to sudden changes in diet. You should also keep treats, chews, and human food to a minimum during this transitional time.

Common Health Problems in Rescued Dogs

Most rescued Greyhounds will arrive in their new home without any health problems as long as you've adopted your new dog from a reputable rescue organization. After a Greyhound has been accepted by a rescue organization, it will likely not be adopted out until any health issues have been resolved. It's not uncommon for Greyhounds to arrive in a rescue with dental problems or flea and tick infestations. In most cases, these dogs will remain in the care of the rescue organization until they are deemed healthy enough to go to their new homes.

Some Greyhounds arrive in rescue after their racing career has ended due to injuries such as damaged tendons or ligaments or broken bones. Again, these problems are generally treated before the dog is approved for adoption, but it's important to be aware of these issues as an adopter. Some injuries can take a long time to heal and may require long-term care or physical therapy in order for the dog to regain normal function. Though these situations are rare, if you are adopting a Greyhound with a history of health problems, it's important to ask about the long-term care required so that you can continue to provide the dog with the right type of care.

CHAPTER 10
Housetraining

Different Options for Housetraining

Housetraining is an important skill for any Greyhound, but the amount of time you spend training will depend on whether you've brought home an adult or a puppy. With a puppy, you'll need to start from scratch as they have small bladders and no knowledge of house rules. Adult Greyhounds, whether coming from a breeder or a rescue organization, may already be housetrained. However, no matter how solid your new dog's housetraining was in his previous home, it's important to understand that he may have a few lapses in training during his first few weeks in his new home. This is a stressful transition, and it's easy for dogs to become confused or over-whelmed and have an accident indoors. Just remember to be patient with your new dog during this time. It can also be helpful to decide how you want to train your Greyhound before you bring him home.

Most Greyhound owners opt to teach their dogs to relieve themselves outside rather than indoors on potty pads or in a litter box. It's also common for owners to teach their Greyhounds to only use a certain area of their outdoor space for going to the bathroom to help preserve the cleanliness of the space for family activities. It's also important to teach your new dog to let you know when he needs to go out. Many dogs quickly learn to alert their owners to their needs by whining, pacing, or pawing at bells placed on the doorknob.

Although potty pads and patches are not recommended for long-term use with Greyhounds, they can be helpful in the housetraining process, espe-cially if you've brought home a puppy. These products give your Greyhound the option of relieving himself in an appropriate area when you aren't avail-able to take him outdoors. Once the dog understands this concept and is old enough to hold it for more than a couple of hours, training can then be shifted to phase out the use of potty pads.

Disposable puppy pads tend to be the most popular choice as you can simply toss the pads in the trash when they've been soiled. However, if you'd prefer less waste, reusable cloth puppy pads are also an option. Reusable pads are made of several layers of fabric, the bottom layer being waterproof and the rest being highly absorbent. Once used, the pads can be laundered in a washing machine and reused again. You may also consider potty patches, which are made of fake grass or turf and can be emptied and washed after use. Any one of these products is a great choice during the first few weeks of housetraining your Greyhound.

Photo Courtesy of
Susan Berthold

The First Few Weeks

During your first few weeks with your new Greyhound, it's important to be patient. Moving into a new household can be overwhelming for some dogs, and it may take them a while to settle in enough to focus on their training. You must also remember to be consistent in both your expectations and training. This will help your dog to understand the rules of the house more quickly.

Greyhounds can be quite sensitive, and punishment at this stage will only serve to damage your relationship with your new dog and stress him out. If you do not catch your Greyhound in the act of relieving himself in the house, you need to just clean up the mess and move on. The age-old advice of "rubbing his nose in it" is inappropriate and will not help your dog learn. Even if you do catch your dog in the act, never hit or spank him. Physical punishment will only serve to frighten him and teach him to go when you're not around.

HELPFUL TIP
Will My Rescue Be Housebroken?

If you're getting ready to bring home a rescued Greyhound, you may be wondering if your dog will be house-trained before coming to you. Most retired racing Greyhounds have only ever lived in a kennel and therefore may not know where to do their business when they arrive at your home, but being intelligent dogs, it shouldn't take long to teach your Greyhound that the bathroom is outside. Mindful use of a crate may assist your efforts. If your rescue dog has been in a foster home, he may have already learned the ins and outs of house-training. However, an accident or two is still par for the course in the early days of introducing any dog into a new home. Be patient and establish clear guidelines early in your relationship, and your rescued Greyhound should be housebroken in no time.

Instead of punishing your Greyhound for his behavior, correct him and move on quickly. If you catch him relieving himself in an inappropriate area, a sharp "No!" or a loud clap or stomp should be enough to interrupt the dog but not scare him. Immediately take him outside and quietly encourage him to continue there. Once he's finished, praise him with plenty of affection and even treats. If you consistently catch him making these mistakes and provide corrections and redirection, your Greyhound will quickly understand what you're trying to tell him.

During your first few weeks with your Greyhound, you'll need to closely manage his environment to be sure that your training can be as consistent as possible. Never let your new dog roam the house unsupervised until you know that he can be trusted not to urinate or defecate indoors. The more frequently he is allowed to do so without correction, the more difficult housetraining will be.

Photo Courtesy of Savannah Peeples

The Importance of Consistency

As stated earlier in the chapter, consistency is key in housetraining your Greyhound. Without consistency, you will both become frustrated at the misunderstanding in your communication. Housetraining requires a lot of attention from everyone in the family, especially with puppies, so it's important that all capable members of the household take responsibility in training the new addition. Every family member should be aware of the new dog's bathroom break schedule and supervision requirements. It's also worthwhile to teach everyone how to respond if they find a mess or catch the dog in the act of relieving himself indoors. You should also make sure that all family members know where the cleaning supplies are and how to properly clean and disinfect the area. For children, this may be as simple as letting an adult know that a mess has been made.

As your Greyhound starts to understand the rules of the house, you can start relaxing your strict reinforcement, but during the first few weeks or months with your new dog, it's important to maintain a fairly strict bathroom schedule. This will help prevent mistakes and encourage a quicker understanding of your expectations. Puppies, especially young ones, will not be able to go more than a couple of hours between bathroom breaks. The same is true for adult Greyhounds that have never been housetrained. You should always be ready to take your dog outside after he eats, naps, or plays.

The best guideline to follow for how often to take your Greyhound outside is based on his age. It's estimated that for every month of your dog's age, he should be able to go for one hour between bathroom breaks. For example, a puppy who is eight weeks old, or about two months, should be able to go no more than two hours before he will need to relieve himself. A four-month-old puppy can be expected to hold it for closer to four hours. Waiting much longer than this almost guarantees an accident. This schedule will need to be kept up around the clock, so you should expect to have relatively sleepless nights for the first few months with your Greyhound puppy. As you get to know him better, you'll be able to adapt the schedule to his individual needs and predict more accurately when he'll need to go out.

If you've rescued an adult Greyhound, it's likely that he has already had housetraining during his time at the track. However, a consistent schedule is needed to make sure that he understands that those same rules apply in his new home. Rescued Greyhounds are used to living with a fairly rigid daily routine, so the more consistency you can provide your new dog, the more quickly he'll settle into his new home.

Positive Reinforcement

Using positive reinforcement in housetraining involves rewarding your dog every time he performs the desired behavior of relieving himself outdoors. With enough repetition, your Greyhound will begin to understand that he can earn the attention or treats that he desires, increasing the likelihood of him repeating the behavior in the future.

As previously mentioned, consistency is key, and this includes building the connection between good behavior and rewards. In the beginning, you'll need to enforce the idea that your Greyhound must relieve himself outdoors before he can have fun. Otherwise, he may only associate your outdoor space with playtime and exploration and potentially forget to go to the bathroom until he comes back inside. Make sure he focuses on the business at hand when you first go outside.

To help your Greyhound understand this concept, remain calm and collected when taking your dog outside. Excitement should be reserved for the reward. Each time your dog relieves himself, you can introduce a verbal command such as "go potty" so that eventually he'll understand what you're telling him to do. Try not to praise your dog too much during the act, as it may interrupt his focus. Once he's finished, celebrate and reward him.

Cleaning Up

When housetraining your Greyhound, you're guaranteed to encounter a few messes. It's important to understand the right way to clean up the mess to ensure that your dog won't feel inclined to repeat himself in the same area. It's also crucial to properly sanitize the area for the health and safety of your entire family.

When shopping for cleaning products, look for products designed specifically for use on pet messes. These products tend to have unique ingredients such as enzymes to help break down the particles responsible for stains and odors. You should also look for products designed for use on the specific types of floors you have in your home. If you have several types of flooring in your home, you may need to invest in more than one cleaning product.

You'll also need to stock up on other cleaning supplies such as towels, scrub brushes, and paper towels. Again, depending on the types of flooring in your home, you may need different tools as well. Paper towels have a tendency to fall apart when scrubbing carpet but work well with hard surface floors such as tile and linoleum. Cloth towels tend to be more durable and can be washed after use rather than thrown away. Scrub brushes also work well with hard flooring, especially when cleaning the grout between tiles. Household steam cleaners are also a popular choice with pet owners whose homes have hard surface flooring. The steam not only helps clean up the mess but also sanitizes the area as well.

Carpeted floors can be especially difficult to clean, so it's important to buy the right product and use the right techniques. You may also want to test the cleaner on an inconspicuous area to make sure it won't discolor the carpet or leave a visible mark. With carpet, it's best to use a soft towel or rag to scrub rather than a brush, as many types of carpet may begin to unravel with vigorous scrubbing with a brush.

Photo Courtesy of
Clair Cuthbertson

Playpens and Doggy Doors

Once you begin to trust your Greyhound more in his housetraining, you can start offering him a bit more freedom. Rather than keeping him in his crate while you're unable to supervise him, you can give him a playpen. A playpen will give your new dog more space to stretch out and play but won't give him enough space to get into trouble. During the early stages of increasing your dog's freedom, you can also line the playpen with disposable or reusable puppy pads. It should be noted that in some cases, playpens are not the ideal solution. Adult Greyhounds and overly rambunctious puppies can easily knock over or escape many types of playpens. With training, they can be taught to respect the boundaries of the playpen, but it may be best to only use the playpen when you're home until you're sure the dog knows to stay inside.

If your outdoor space is safe enough and you trust your Greyhound with more freedom, you can also consider investing in a doggy door. Doggy doors give your dog more control over his own bathroom schedule, which generally means fewer accidents in the house. Doggy doors may be temporarily or permanently installed in your home. If you would prefer a temporary installation, or you're a renter, you might consider types of doors that can be easily installed into sliding patio doors without damaging or changing the structure of the door. If you'd prefer a more permanent solution, doggy doors can be installed in most types of doors or walls. Many types of doggy doors can also be locked to prevent intruders from entering the house while you're away. Some doors also require your dog to wear a tag on his collar to unlock the door as he approaches. This can help prevent other pets from leaving the house through the door as well as preventing neighborhood strays or wild animals from entering.

No matter what type of door you choose, make sure it's the right size for your Greyhound. If your Greyhound is still a puppy, you might want to consider a temporary door until he reaches his adult size or buy a door that will be big enough for him once he's fully grown. If you're unsure of how big your dog will be as an adult, you can usually estimate based on breed averages.

If you're considering giving your Greyhound the additional freedom of a playpen or doggy door, you need to be sure that he's ready for that responsibility. If he's not, it could set your housetraining back, or he could get himself into serious trouble. You will also need to make sure your Greyhound is getting enough physical and mental exercise to make sure that he won't feel the need to entertain himself in your absence.

CHAPTER 11
Socialization

The Importance of Good Socialization

One of the most important benefits to socializing your Greyhound is that you will be able to confidently take him anywhere, knowing that you'll be able to predict how he behaves in new situations. As you socialize your new dog, he will become more confident in unfamiliar environments, and you will begin to gain confidence in his behavior. If you plan on showing or competing with your Greyhound, this is especially important. However, even

Photo Courtesy of
Susie Morris

if you only want to take your Greyhound for the occasional weekend hike or trip to the local café, he will need to be socialized so that these events won't cause him stress.

When socializing your Greyhound, it's important to understand that socialization is not a one-time event. It must be done constantly throughout your dog's lifetime to ensure that he will always approach new situations with confidence and trust in you.

It must also be noted that socialization is commonly approached as introducing your dog to as many new people and dogs as possible in a short amount of time. While meeting new people and pets is important, too many introductions too quickly can cause your dog to become uncertain and even fearful. Rather, socialization should consist of exposing your dog to new situations while still respecting his comfort zone. If your Greyhound is uncomfortable meeting new dogs, take him places where he can watch other dogs from afar and approach as he feels comfortable. Socialization is not about forcing your dog to do things he doesn't want to. Instead, it's about giving your dog the confidence to handle himself wherever you take him.

You can also socialize your dog at home by exposing him to new sights, sounds, scents, and feelings. Use household items like hair dryers, blenders, and vacuums to get your Greyhound used to loud, unfamiliar noises. Have him walk over unusual surfaces like tarps, pieces of wood, or even bubble wrap. Handle your dog to get him used to the way he'll be handled by groomers and vets. Most importantly, begin teaching him coping behaviors such as focusing on you during times of discomfort.

Socializing Puppies

If you're purchasing your new Greyhound from a reputable breeder, it's likely that socialization has already begun before you even bring your puppy home. Socialization methods such as Puppy Culture allow breeders to prepare their puppies for life in their new homes. It's your responsibility to continue this process once you welcome your new Greyhound home.

However, caution must be taken when socializing young puppies outside the home. Puppies under the age of 16 weeks are not fully vaccinated, and it's generally not considered a good idea to take them in public where they may be exposed to dangerous pathogens. Until your Greyhound has been fully vaccinated, which typically happens around

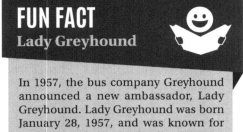

FUN FACT

Lady Greyhound

In 1957, the bus company Greyhound announced a new ambassador, Lady Greyhound. Lady Greyhound was born January 28, 1957, and was known for her diamond tiara and collar. In 1963, she had a fashion show at the New York World's Fair. The Lady Greyhound campaign came to an end in 1970.

the age of 16 weeks, it's best to keep your puppy at home. Most home environments provide plenty of opportunities for socialization. If you have an outdoor space, such as a yard, you can use that to introduce your puppy to the outside world, just on a smaller scale. Even just having your puppy feel concrete, soil, or wood planks under his feet will help to prepare him for the world outside.

As previously mentioned, handling is an important part of the socialization process and should be started as soon as possible. The more you can handle your puppy at home, the less afraid he'll be when the groomer trims his nails or the vet examines him for the first time. Be sure to handle his feet and toes, as well as other potentially sensitive areas such as his ears and mouth. If you plan on trimming your puppy's nails or brushing his teeth at home, now is a great time to introduce him to these sensations.

Once your vet has fully vaccinated your Greyhound, you can build on the foundation of socialization that you started at home. Start small and explore the area around your home and neighborhood. Take your puppy for brief car rides or walks around the local park. If you have friends with puppies, set up puppy playdates to help your dog with his understanding of canine body language and appropriate behavior. During this delicate stage of socialization, most experts recommend avoiding the dog park. Dog parks can be overwhelming for a nervous puppy, and accidents can happen quickly. Instead, you might consider signing up for a puppy obedience class. Many obedience classes allow some playtime in a safe, supervised environment.

Though you should expose your Greyhound puppy to as many new experiences as possible, it's important to avoid overwhelming him. As his owner, it's your responsibility to look out for his well-being, both physically and mentally. You need to ensure that his socialization consists of positive experiences. Even a single bad experience can set your training back by months, so proceed cautiously. If you notice nervous or fearful body language from your puppy, remove him from the situation and try again later. As he becomes more confident, you can help him learn to work through his fear, but in the moment is not the time.

Socializing Adult Dogs

Though many owners adopt adult Greyhounds thinking it will be easier than raising a puppy, in many ways, socialization is the same with dogs of any age. The downside of socializing adults is that you may not be fully aware of the dog's past experiences, and it may be more difficult to predict how your dog will react in new situations. Some dogs may have past trauma that you are not aware of, and it will only become evident during socialization and training.

When socializing adult Greyhounds, it's just as important as it is with puppies to ensure your dog has only good experiences. Approach new situations slowly and give him time to adjust. During this time, you're earning his trust, and he may have little confidence. Try approaching situations from afar and only moving closer when your dog seems comfortable. Again, it may be best to avoid dog parks and instead introduce him only to dogs you know and trust at first. Most rescued adult Greyhounds are used to living in a pack environment at the track, so they tend to get along well with other dogs, but it's still best to be careful. If you're unsure of how a new dog will react to your Greyhound, it may be best to avoid interaction altogether.

If your Greyhound has had negative experiences in his past that you are aware of, you'll have a better idea of what areas of socialization to approach with extra caution. For some dogs, it can take months or even years of work to overcome past trauma. It can be easy to become frustrated with a dog's lack of progress in these situations, but it's crucial to stay patient and consistent.

Socialization and Former Racing Dogs

Most rescued Greyhounds are fairly well socialized due to their experiences at the track. They are housed near many other dogs and usually have good social skills. They are frequently handled by trainers, assistants, caretakers, and track veterinarians. As a result, these dogs tend to be quite confident in situations where they encounter new dogs and people. However, it's important to note that almost all of the dogs a Greyhound will meet during his time at the track will be other Greyhounds. Your Greyhound may be unfamiliar with dogs of other breeds, shapes, and sizes. He will need slow introductions to other types of animals such as cats, pocket pets, or livestock. Additionally, life in a home rather than in a kennel will be completely new to him. For this reason, it's essential that you're prepared to be patient with your new Greyhound. Socialization should be approached slowly during your first few months together. As your Greyhound gains trust in you and confidence in himself, you can begin challenging him more.

Lifelong Socialization

As you socialize your Greyhound and build the bond between you, you can begin exposing him to situations where he may be fearful or nervous. These experiences can be traumatic during the early stages of socialization, but eventually, you must teach your dog to trust you and work through his

Photo Courtesy of
Blazka Ribic

fear. Once your dog understands that you'll never put him in a situation where he is in danger, he'll be less likely to panic or shut down when he's afraid. However, it's also important to avoid exposing him to too many frightening situations. Socialization must be performed correctly and consistently throughout your Greyhound's lifetime in order to maintain that level of trust and confidence.

One of the most beneficial aspects of good socialization throughout your Greyhound's life is that it will make training and exercising your dog much easier. The more comfortable he is in new situations, the more you can do with him. A well-socialized dog will be comfortable competing at a new venue, hiking an unfamiliar trail, or relaxing on a cross-country road trip. The more places you can take your Greyhound, the more opportunities he has to exercise his mind and body.

Dealing with High Prey Drives

As with many sighthounds, it's common for Greyhounds to have high prey drives. This applies to both rescued Greyhounds and those purchased from a reputable breeder. However, each dog is an individual, and while one Greyhound may go wild every time it sees a squirrel, another may be uninterested. This can make it difficult to trust a dog around small animals such as cats, small dogs, or pocket pets. It is also the reason most Greyhound experts recommend that you never allow your dog off-leash in an unfenced area. Your Greyhound may spot a rabbit in the distance and be so focused on the pursuit that he doesn't realize he's running toward a busy road or other potentially dangerous area.

While it's unlikely that you're ever going to be able to eliminate your Greyhound's prey drive, you can teach him to control it. If you've brought home a puppy, begin teaching him appropriate behavior around small animals as soon as possible. With adult dogs, you may need to be more cautious about how you introduce them to small animals, but the sooner you can start working on it, the better.

A great command to teach your Greyhound is "watch me" or "focus." This can be helpful in teaching your dog to focus on you rather than the neighborhood squirrels. To teach this command, start by working with him in a low-distraction environment such as your home. Wave a treat in front of his face to get his attention and move the treat in front of your face. When he looks at you, reward him. As he begins to understand your expectations, you can introduce a verbal command. With practice, you can start working with him outside as well as in more distracting environments.

If you plan on competing with your Greyhound in coursing competitions, your dog's prey drive will be essential to his success. Though the lure in these competitions is typically a plastic bag rather than a live animal, your dog sees the pursuit the same way. His prey drive will need to be encouraged, but you can also help him to understand when it's appropriate to chase and when it isn't. Your Greyhound will be able to easily differentiate between the vest and muzzle worn while coursing and the collar or harness you normally walk him in. As long as you remain consistent in your training, he will be able to understand that he's allowed to get excited about chasing the lure, but he needs to leave the neighbor's cat alone.

Depending on your Greyhound's prey drive, you may also need to accept that your dog will never be able to be safely left alone with small animals or allowed off-leash in unfenced areas. Some dogs have too strong of a drive to see smaller creatures as anything but prey. If this is the case with your dog, you need to carefully manage his environment to avoid any situations where he could injure or even kill another animal.

Photo Courtesy of Deborah FitzGerald

Dealing with Fear

No matter how hard you try to avoid overwhelming your Greyhound, you will eventually find yourself in a situation where your dog feels afraid. You should be prepared for these events so that you know how to handle them and don't accidentally encourage your dog's fearful reactions. These situations are important learning opportunities for both you and your dog. Rather than allowing the situation to leave a negative impression on your dog, you can teach him to trust you and work through his fear.

The first step is to recognize fearful body language. Nervous or fearful Greyhounds may tuck their tail under their bodies and flatten their ears. They may also pant, tremble, yawn, lick their lips, and avoid eye contact. These behaviors typically indicate a mild fearful reaction, and most dogs can be distracted or calmed down at this point. However, if the issue isn't addressed, the dog may panic and attempt to escape. Panicked dogs may also lash out aggressively if they feel threatened, so it's important to address the fear at the first sign.

The most important aspect of teaching your Greyhound to work through his fear is keeping your own reaction under control. If you get nervous too, your dog will understand that there is a good reason to be afraid, and his behavior may escalate. By remaining calm and collected, you're telling your dog that you have everything under control, and he has nothing to worry about. Do not coddle or attempt to comfort your dog during times of fear. He will likely interpret this as reassurance that he should be afraid. However, harsh corrections will not work either, as they may overstimulate him to the point of panic. Instead, remain calm and speak in a level tone. Try to set a good example for your dog and reward him once he begins to relax.

Once the situation is over, you can reflect on the reactions of you and your Greyhound. Think about what you could have done differently to improve the situation. If you were able to successfully calm your dog down and help him through his fear, you might be able to look back and know you did everything right. However, if the situation went differently than you were expecting, consider what you can do next time to get a more positive result. If you consistently struggle with helping your Greyhound through his fear, contact a professional trainer or canine behaviorist. Fear issues can be difficult to work through, especially for inexperienced owners. The sooner you can seek professional help, the sooner you and your dog will be on the path to success.

CHAPTER 12

The Multi-pet Household

Introducing a Puppy to Other Animals

Unless your new Greyhound puppy is your only pet, you're going to need to properly introduce him to the rest of your household. In most cases, it's not the puppy you need to worry about but your existing pets. Puppies are usually enthusiastic about meeting new friends, but some may be more nervous than others. Even if your current pets are typically friendly toward other animals, it's best to be cautious during introductions to make sure everyone's boundaries are respected, and no one gets hurt.

When introducing your new Greyhound to your current pets, proper restraint will be necessary to keep all animals safe. For most dogs, a collar and leash will be fine, but if your puppy isn't yet used to a collar or pulling is a concern, a harness may also be used. Harnesses are also a good choice because if you suspect your puppy may be in danger, you can quickly grab his harness and remove him from the situation without worrying about damaging his neck by pulling suddenly on his collar. For cats, it's usually best to restrain the puppy and allow the cats to move around freely. For pocket pets, poultry, or livestock, a fence or cage barrier is recommended. However, even if your other animals are safe behind a fence, it's best to keep your Greyhound on a leash to avoid the temptation of climbing through the fence or chasing animals along the fence line.

As you begin introductions, be sure to go slowly. Start by allowing the animals plenty of space between them. If they seem comfortable, you can move them closer, but if at any time they appear nervous or uncomfortable, do not move them closer together. In most cases, introducing the animals on neutral territory outside the home is ideal. Outdoor spaces also allow more space to move away than most houses. You'll need to monitor all animals' body language to ensure that they are not experiencing fear, anxiety, or aggression. If you notice signs of these emotions, you need to separate the animals immediately or give them more space. For particularly nervous animals, you may need to hold several introductory sessions before they feel comfortable around the new addition.

During the first few months with your Greyhound puppy, you need to make sure that he is never left unsupervised with your other pets. Accidents can happen quickly, even if you think everyone is getting along, so it's important to keep an eye on them until you're completely sure that it's safe to trust them.

Photo Courtesy of
Hazel McIntyre

Introducing an Adult Dog to Other Animals

If you've adopted an adult Greyhound, you'll need to use the same caution you would when introducing a puppy to your existing pets. However,
there are a few key differences in introducing adult dogs to new animals,
especially if their past is relatively unknown. Unless you know for a fact that
your new Greyhound has been properly socialized around the same species
as your current pets, you need to be more aware of your new dog's body
language. With puppies, most of your focus will be on your other animals,
but with adult dogs, you need to watch their body language as well in order
to prioritize everyone's safety. An adult Greyhound can quickly catch and
injure another animal, so it's also important to properly restrain all animals
in the introduction. Be sure that whoever is holding your Greyhound's leash
is strong enough to keep the dog under control should he lunge at or try to
chase the other animal.

Just as you would with a puppy, you need to start at a distance and move
slowly to avoid frightening either your Greyhound or the other pet. If your
Greyhound reacts aggressively toward your other animal, it may be best to
consult a trainer or behaviorist to help you with introductions. Otherwise,
your pets' safety could be at risk.

Greyhounds and Small Pets

Generally, if you are getting your adult dog from a reputable breeder
or foster home, you should be able to ask about the dog's prey drive and
past experiences with small animals. If you have cats and the dog has been
deemed to be unsafe around cats, it's unlikely you'll be allowed to adopt the
dog. However, it's possible that you may be adopting a Greyhound with an
unknown history around small animals. Prey drive can be seen in puppies,
but it's generally more manageable, and the dog can be taught not to chase.

Regardless of what you've been told about your new Greyhound, it's
essential that you introduce him to your small pets with extreme caution. A
dog's prey drive is typically triggered by sudden movement, so if the small
pet gets frightened and moves away suddenly, your Greyhound may give
chase. This is why proper restraint is so important. You won't have a chance
at catching your Greyhound once he's on the run, so you need to make sure
you have control over him at all times.

It's important to remember that you may never be able to let your
Greyhound near your small pets. It's not uncommon for owners to keep
their dogs away from small pets like rabbits or chickens at all times. It can

Photo Courtesy of
Bianca King

be more difficult with animals that share your home, such as cats, but it's not impossible. If you aren't up to the challenge of this type of lifestyle management, consult a professional trainer or behaviorist for advice.

Fighting and Bad Behavior

Greyhounds are not typically a breed known for aggression, but this does not mean it's not a potential problem. Aggression is a serious behavioral problem that needs to be addressed at the first sign. Otherwise, your pets may be at risk of serious injuries, which can be potentially fatal. Nearly all dogs will display some type of warning sign prior to attacking another animal, so it's important that you are able to recognize these signs and correct the behavior as soon as possible. Dog fights are dangerous to your dogs as well as any humans that try to intervene, especially if there is a significant size difference. Greyhounds are large dogs that are capable of serious damage. On the flip side, this breed also tends to have quite thin skin, and they can be seriously injured in a fight.

Most fights are triggered by behaviors such as resource guarding or bullying. These behaviors should not be tolerated, no matter which animal is displaying the behavior. Though dogs should be allowed to have some personal boundaries, they shouldn't be allowed to push each other around or claim items such as toys, furniture, or people. Generally, an interruption such as a loud clap or "No!" will be enough to draw your dogs' attention to you instead of each other.

In order to spot aggressive behavior in its early stages, you need to be on the lookout for aggressive body language. Aggressive dogs tend to stand tall with their heads high above the other dog. The body will be tense, and the dominant dog may lean forward slightly toward the other animal. Intense eye contact, bared teeth, and raised hackles are also signs of aggression. Note that some dogs will not display such obvious signs before attacking. It may be as subtle as a stiffened posture and direct eye contact, but you need to understand your dog's body language well enough to know when to intervene. If this behavior is not stopped immediately, a fight is imminent.

You should also be on the lookout for obvious triggers to your dogs' aggressive behavior. Rough play, bullying, or dominant behavior are common causes. If your dog has trouble sharing his food or toys or guards certain pieces of furniture or people, you'll better be able to solve the problem once you know what's triggering his aggression. Resource guarding can be a difficult problem to solve for inexperienced owners, so if you're not sure how to proceed, it's best to consult a professional as soon as possible.

If your dogs' aggressive behavior does result in a fight, you need to be extremely cautious when breaking it up. Even dogs that are normally friendly towards people may redirect their aggression and bite anyone who tries to come between them and the dog they're fighting. Never try to separate the dogs by grabbing their collars or bodies. Some fights can be broken up with little effort, while others may be more difficult to stop.

This is one of the only occasions where it is appropriate to yell at your dogs. Stomping, clapping, or banging metal dog bowls together can also be used to stop the fight. You may also consider throwing a bowl of water at the dogs or spraying them with a hose if it's nearby. Throwing a blanket over the dogs may also be disorienting enough to stop them.

If you absolutely must intervene, you need to first decide which dog is the aggressor and which dog is defending himself. If you have two people available, each of you needs to choose a dog to restrain. If you are alone, you need to choose the aggressor. Grab the dog by the back legs and either pull him backwards quickly or swing him to the side. This move needs to be done quickly to avoid the dog redirecting his aggression onto you. Once the dogs are separated, quickly restrain them before they can resume the fight.

It's important to note that on occasion, dogs will bite down onto each other and refuse to let go. If this happens, you should never try to pry their jaws open with your bare hands. This will certainly end in a bite. Instead, use a sturdy wedge-shaped object to pry their jaws apart. If you're worried about this happening, you can invest in a product called a break stick, which is a wedge of wood or plastic designed to pry open a dog's mouth. If you use a break stick, make sure your hands are far enough from the dog's mouth when you use it that you can avoid being bitten if the dog tries to regrip.

Aggression, especially once it has escalated to actual fights, can be a difficult behavior problem for the average owner to address on their own. Any time your dog begins to display aggressive behavior, it's recommended to seek professional help immediately. A professional trainer or veterinary behaviorist will be more equipped to address the problem

HELPFUL TIP
Camping

Camping with your dog can be a fun and rewarding experience, but it's important to take some cautionary steps to ensure a safe and enjoyable time. It's important to discuss vaccinations with your vet before embarking on an outdoor adventure since diseases such as leptospirosis may be more easily contracted at your destination. Be sure to bring the appropriate receptacle for disposing of your pet's waste, and double-check that your dog is up to date with preventive measures for fleas, ticks, and heartworm.

lem and prevent you or your dogs from getting injured in a fight.

Raising Multiple Puppies from the Same Litter

If you don't have other dogs at home, you may consider adopting more than one puppy at a time. This may seem like an ideal situation since your new Greyhounds will always have a companion and playmate by their side. However, in reality, raising multiple puppies from the same litter is an incredibly difficult task for even experienced dog owners. In addition to spending more time training and cleaning up after multiple puppies, it can be difficult to prevent them from developing littermate syndrome. Littermate syndrome is a group of behaviors that can be developed by dogs of the same age raised in the same household. Despite the name, it is not strictly limited to littermates and can be developed by any group of puppies close in age. It's common for at least one of the puppies to become withdrawn or introverted, while another tends to be more of a bully. The puppies are usually so co-dependent that they may panic if separated. Puppies with littermate syndrome tend to bond more closely to each other than their humans, which can interfere with training. Eventually, littermate syndrome can lead to aggression and even fighting between the puppies.

Due to the common problem of littermate syndrome, few reputable breeders will allow an owner to take home more than one puppy. If you're seeking a solution to your new Greyhound being left home alone, it's best

to focus your efforts on training your puppy and eliminating separation anxiety. Once your puppy has matured a bit and is relatively well trained, you can consider bringing home a companion for him. This way, your puppy will have time to bond with you and learn the rules of the household. This will allow you to focus on the second puppy once he arrives without worrying too much about the first.

Options if Your Pets Don't Get Along

One of the risks you face in a multi-pet home is your pets not getting along, no matter how hard you try. Though Greyhounds generally do well in a pack setting, it's possible that your new dog may not get along with your existing pets. Likewise, it's also possible that your existing pets may not accept a new addition. Older pets, in particular, can be resistant to change, so it's important that you give them plenty of time to adapt before making any serious decisions. Patience and commitment are essential in helping animals adapt to living in a group setting, but you may consider seeking professional help if you're struggling.

Unfortunately, no matter how hard you try, some pets may simply refuse to get along. This may force you to make a heartbreaking decision. If you choose to keep two pets that don't get along, you'll need to carefully manage their lives in a way that keeps them separated at all times. With small animals such as rabbits or cats, this may not be too difficult, but with large dogs, it can be a hassle to constantly crate and rotate them or section off your home. You'll need to do all this while also making sure each dog has enough physical and mental stimulation, affection, and care. You'll need to make sure each dog has a comfortable space they can call their own while the other is out. In some cases, you may need to avoid all contact between the two animals. This can be incredibly exhausting and time-consuming, and few owners can provide this type of living environment. If your pets aren't getting along, you need to seriously consider whether you are able to provide this type of care for your pets' entire lives.

If you are unable or unwilling to provide your pets with completely separate care, there's no shame in rehoming a dog as long as it's in the dog's best interest to do so. Some pets prefer to be the only animal in the home, while others may simply need a different environment to thrive. Though this decision can be heartbreaking, it's important to advocate for your animals' overall wellbeing. No matter how much you love your pets, if you are not able to provide them with the ideal lifestyle, it's your responsibility to ensure that they go to the right kind of home. As your animals' caretaker, the greatest thing you can do for your pets is to make sure they're happy and well cared for.

CHAPTER 13
Training Your Greyhound

Training the Greyhound

Training your Greyhound will be an essential part of your daily routine. However, it's important to note that Greyhounds are not the easiest breed to train. They are incredibly sensitive dogs that need to be trained with a gentle touch. Additionally, they can be quite stubborn, so training sessions will need to be short and interesting enough for the dog to enjoy.

With proper training, your Greyhound will not only become a well-behaved member of the family, but you'll also be able to take him with you on errands or vacation, knowing that you can trust him to behave himself in public. A well-trained Greyhound is an ambassador to the breed and will surely make an impression wherever you go. Training sessions are also a great way to keep your Greyhound's mind active, especially for puppies and senior dogs who may have physical limitations. Whether you're teaching your Greyhound basic obedience or fun and entertaining tricks, you'll be strengthening the bond between you and your beloved companion.

HELPFUL TIP
Positive Reinforcement

Greyhounds typically have quiet, sensitive demeanors, making them well suited for a variety of households. However, this sensitive nature makes it imperative that any training methodology you choose to follow relies on positive rather than negative reinforcement. An example of positive reinforcement training includes giving your dog a treat, praise, or petting each time he completes the desired task. The reward helps your dog equate the completed task with a desirable outcome. Negative reinforcement can create anxiety in any dog, but particularly those with more sensitive natures.

Photo Courtesy of Karen Robertson

Training Adults vs. Puppies

In many ways, training an adult Greyhound is similar to training a puppy. However, there are some key differences to keep in mind. First, puppies will generally have a shorter attention span than adults, so you'll need to keep training sessions especially short. Three-to-five-minute sessions are ideal for keeping the dog engaged but without the risk of losing focus.

With adult Greyhounds, it's important to consider the fact that though they may be fairly well socialized, living in a house may be an unfamiliar experience. Unless the dog has spent a significant amount of time in a foster home, you will likely need to start from scratch in terms of training. Adults will be able to withstand longer training sessions than puppies, but you should still keep them fairly short so that your dog stays focused and engaged. This will also encourage him to look forward to the next session rather than dread it.

Operant Conditioning Basics

Operant conditioning is one of the most popular learning methods used by professional dog trainers. This method was originally coined and promoted by American psychologist and behaviorist B.F. Skinner. He based his theories on the idea that both humans and animals are too complex to learn through just classical conditioning. He theorized that as long as behaviors were followed by positive experiences, the learner would be more likely to perform the behavior again. If certain behaviors were followed by negative experiences, the learner would be discouraged from repeating the behavior in the future.

Skinner described three types of environmental responses that can shape an animal or human's behavior: neutral operants, reinforcers, and punishments. As the name suggests, neutral operants are environmental responses that are neutral to the learner. That is, they have no influence on whether a learner will repeat a particular behavior. For example, if your dog barks and you respond by ignoring him, you are considered a neutral operant as your behavior will not influence the likelihood of your dog barking in the future. Reinforcers, on the other hand, will encourage a learner to repeat a certain behavior. Reinforcers can be either positive or negative.

Positive reinforcers include rewards such as food, praise, playtime, and affection. Positive reinforcement is the most common method of training dogs of any breed. Most dogs are easily motivated by food, toys, or affection, so it's typically one of the most effective methods available to teach a dog new commands. However, it's important to note that bad behaviors can also be learned through positive reinforcement. If a dog shoves his way out the front door and is rewarded with an exciting sprint through the neighborhood, he's more likely to shove his way out again. The same goes for getting into the trash. If the dog finds delicious treats in the trash can, he's more likely to dig through the trash in the future. To prevent your dog from engaging in self-rewarding behavior, you must manage your Greyhound's environment closely to make sure he doesn't have the opportunity.

Negative reinforcers are not to be confused with punishments. Negative reinforcement is commonly looked down upon by uninformed dog owners, but this is only because they have confused the concept with punishment. Negative reinforcement is the removal of an unpleasant sensation, such as gentle pressure on the leash or a hand on the dog's body. It is typically combined with positive reinforcement to further encourage a dog to perform the correct behavior. An example of negative reinforcement occurs during leash training. You put gentle pressure on the leash to encourage your dog to follow you. At first, he's likely to brace against the pressure, so you maintain it until the moment he steps toward you. Once he moves in the correct direction, you can reward him by removing the pressure on the leash. This concept can then be combined with positive reinforcement by rewarding the dog with food, praise, or a toy.

By contrast, punishments are the introduction of an unpleasant sensation in response to a behavior and will discourage a learner from repeating the behavior in the future. Punishments may be slightly unpleasant, such as a sharp "No!" For example, if you catch your dog doing something naughty, you might give him a verbal correction or stomp your feet or clap your hands to distract him. These sounds do not hurt him, but they aren't pleasant, and with repetition, they will generally be enough to discourage him from performing the behavior again.

Painful punishments should never be used on any dog, as they can permanently affect the dog's behavior around humans as well as cause serious physical injuries. Never hit, kick, or scream at your Greyhound. Greyhounds are incredibly sensitive dogs and generally need only gentle corrections. In addition to the risk of having the dog lash out when frightened, you risk leaving your dog with lasting mental or physical trauma. Even if your dog is fighting or displaying aggressive behavior, hitting and kicking your dog is unacceptable.

Photo Courtesy of Bianca King

Essential Commands

Though few Greyhounds wish to perform advanced obedience commands, it's entirely possible to teach your dog many useful skills. With patience and consistency, a Greyhound can easily learn enough commands to make life easier. This foundation can then be built on as your dog progresses. Whether you just intend to have an active companion or want a future show ring or sports competitor, your Greyhound is going to need to know basic skills such as walking nicely on the leash and recognizing his own name, though he still may not respond when distracted by one of the neighborhood squirrels.

Name Recognition

If you're bringing home an adult Greyhound, it's possible that he may already recognize his given name. However, if you've adopted a puppy or want to change your Greyhound's name, you'll need to condition him to respond to his new name. Name recognition is a basic skill that will be used throughout your dog's life, so it's a great place to start your training.

At first, you will need to keep your Greyhound on a leash to prevent him from wandering off, especially if he's distracted or not highly food motivated. Gain your Greyhound's attention by waving a treat in front of his nose. Once he's focused on you, say his name, and immediately give him the treat along with a marker word such as "good" or "yes." Repeat this process a few times and be sure to reward him each time you say his name. Training sessions for this particular skill don't need to be long but more frequent sessions will work best. With enough repetition, your Greyhound will understand that when you say his name, he needs to pay attention to you as there may be a tasty reward waiting for him if he responds appropriately.

Sit

After name recognition, sit is usually the second command taught to most dogs as it is quite easy to teach. Whether you're asking your Greyhound to wait politely while you put on his collar and leash, or you want to try your hand at dog sports, the sit command is one that you'll frequently find useful. As mentioned earlier, you can use either positive reinforcement alone or a combination of positive and negative reinforcement. Some dogs learn better with both, while others do better with just positive reinforcement. Only you will be able to determine which method your Greyhound prefers.

Again, you'll want to have your Greyhound wear his collar and leash to prevent him from walking away should he get distracted. Wave a treat in front of his face or say his name to gain his attention. Once he's focused on you, lure him into a sitting position by holding the treat above his head. It may take a moment for him to understand that the treat is best reached by sitting rather than jumping up, but it's important to remain patient while he figures it out. No verbal command is required at this point. Once your Greyhound's hind end touches the ground, reward him immediately. As your dog begins to understand what you're asking, you can start introducing the verbal command.

To add negative reinforcement to your training session, you have two options. The first involves applying gentle pressure above your dog's hips with one hand while you lure him into position with the other. When your Greyhound's hind end is as close to the ground as it can get, immediately release the pressure and give him a reward. If you'd prefer not to use pressure on the hind end, you can also apply gentle upwards pressure on the leash. Again, when your Greyhound performs the correct behavior, release the pressure immediately and reward him. Timing is crucial when using negative reinforcement, so be sure to release the pressure as soon as the dog moves in the right direction.

Lie Down

The lie-down command is useful for any dog, and the sit command can be used as the foundation for teaching this skill. You can use lie down to ask your dog to rest while you have lunch at the local café or while you're traveling in the car. As with sit, lie down is also used in a variety of dog sports should you choose to compete with your Greyhound.

Your Greyhound does not need to know how to sit before you teach him to lie down, but it can be helpful to place your dog in a sitting position to start. Consider having your Greyhound on a collar and leash to prevent him from walking away. Gain his attention with a treat and lure him down to the ground into a lying position. Some dogs will stand up or simply put their heads down rather than lying down, but it's important to remain patient. You may want to move the treat down and slightly ahead of the dog to encourage him to lie down. If he moves out of position, simply ask him to sit and try again. Once his elbows touch the ground, you can reward him.

If you'd like to use negative reinforcement to teach the down command, you can also put gentle downward pressure on the leash as you lure your Greyhound into position. If your dog attempts to move away or brace against the pressure, just maintain that same amount of gentle pressure. Do not attempt to pull your dog down or increase the pressure. The key to this method is to use gentle but flexible tension on the leash. Never stand on the leash as this creates more pressure than just using your hand, and your dog could panic. With patience and tasty treats, your Greyhound will eventually understand what you're asking, and when his elbows touch the floor, you can immediately release the pressure and reward him.

Stay

The stay or wait command can be useful for any Greyhound and helps teach the dog patience and respect. It's also a required skill in many dog sports. It should be noted that many trainers differentiate between wait and stay, while others use these terms interchangeably. For handlers that choose to differentiate, stay is typically reserved for longer periods of time and requires that the handler return to their original position to release the dog. Wait is used for short periods of time, and the handler may release the dog at a distance, such as during recall practice.

Though stay can technically be performed in any position, you should start with whichever position your Greyhound is most comfortable in. Most dogs will try to walk away the first few times they try to stand while staying, so it may be helpful to start with the dog either sitting or lying down. Once your dog is in position, you can give him the verbal command along with a hand signal if you choose. Wait just a moment and reward your Greyhound for staying in position. You can use a verbal command to release him, such as "ok" or "free" as well. If he moves before you release him, simply put him back into position and try again. As your dog's understanding of the command increases, you can try taking a step or two away or increase the duration of the stay. For advanced training, you can also introduce distractions such as other people or dogs, tossing treats or toys, or leaving the room entirely.

Recall

Recall is one of the most important commands to teach any dog. However, it's worth mentioning that no matter how frequently you work on your Greyhound's recall, it's always possible that he may ignore you once he's in pursuit of a small prey animal. This does not reflect negatively on your training; it's simply a result of your sighthound's instincts overruling his conditioning. For this reason, no matter how good your Greyhound's recall training is, you should always keep him on a leash in unfenced areas.

To teach your Greyhound to come when he is called, you may want to have a friend or family member help you. It will also be helpful to start in a quiet, familiar area such as your home or backyard. Wherever you choose to practice, make sure the area is fenced, or you have your Greyhound on a long leash.

Have your helper hold your dog while you walk a short distance away. Say your dog's name to gain his attention and excitedly ask him to come to you using a high-pitched voice and plenty of clapping or patting your legs. Have your helper hold the Greyhound back for just a moment while you do this to help build your dog's excitement. The helper can then release the dog while he runs to you.

Photo Courtesy of Saffi Karim

As your dog runs to you, you can also run backward a few steps to further encourage him to play this new and exciting game. Once the dog reaches you, you can repeat the process by having your helper call the dog back. This can be repeated a few times but be sure to quit before your Greyhound gets tired or loses focus. Short, frequent sessions are better than marathon training sessions as they will keep your dog more engaged and eager to learn.

Off

The off command is used to teach your Greyhound to move off of the furniture when you ask. While some owners may discourage their dogs from getting on the furniture at all, others simply need their dogs to get out of the way on occasion. For this command, it's important to use a specific word such as "off" rather than "down" or "get down" as the dog may confuse your request with "lie down" or "down." The exact words you use don't matter, so long as you're willing to use them consistently and in the correct context.

If your Greyhound is familiar with the concept of luring, you can use his favorite treats to lure him off the furniture while introducing the verbal command of your choice. Once the dog's four feet are all firmly on the floor, you can reward him with the treat and plenty of affection.

You can also use negative reinforcement, though this may not be appropriate for all dogs. The first method of introducing negative reinforcement is to keep a collar and a short drag leash on your dog in the house. When he gets onto the furniture, you can lure him off with a treat while also applying gentle pressure on the leash in the direction you want him to go. Again, reward when the dog's four feet are all on the ground.

You can also use your hand to either grab the collar or push on your Greyhound's rear with gentle pressure, but it should be noted that this isn't safe with all dogs. Some dogs, especially fearful dogs or those with resource guarding issues, may try to snap at your hands. For these types of dogs, it's recommended to use luring only or luring with a collar and leash to keep your hands at a safe distance. If you do use the leash method, it's important that you remember to remove the collar and leash when you leave your Greyhound home alone. If left attached, your dog could easily hurt himself with the leash or chew it up and swallow it.

Drop It

The drop-it command is an important skill for dogs to have both at home and away. At any time, your Greyhound might pick up something questionable, so you need to teach him to drop it right away. This is a much safer method of dealing with this problem rather than racing to take a possibly dangerous object out of your dog's mouth before he swallows it.

Taking objects from your Greyhound's mouth is never recommended. Though most Greyhounds are easygoing enough to tolerate it, some Greyhounds may snap at you. It's also possible that your dog will clamp his jaws around whatever it is you're trying to take and refuse to let go. The best way to get the object out of his mouth is by trading. For this, you'll need to use high-value treats, such as meat or even small bits of cheese.

Offer your Greyhound the new item but try to lure his head away from the object you're trying to take. As he drops the item, give the verbal command, and get ready to grab the item as soon as his face is a safe distance away. Practice with items he's allowed to have, like toys or chews. This way, after you've traded, simply give him back the item and try again.

Leave It

As with the drop-it command, leave it is ideal for keeping your Greyhound out of trouble. Whether it's an overly nosy neighbor dog or a fallen French fry, a solid leave-it command will teach your dog to walk away from whatever it is he might get into trouble with. Again, you'll need to use high-value rewards to ensure that your Greyhound is more interested in what you have than whatever it is that is distracting him. You can use whatever phrase you want for this command, but most trainers use "leave it" or "walk away" or something similar.

When your Greyhound gets distracted by something on the ground or in the distance, wave a high-value treat in front of his face and lure him in the opposite direction while giving a verbal command. When this is done with an appropriately tasty treat, your dog should readily refocus on you. At first, you may only be able to get him to turn away from the distraction, but eventually, you can ask him to take a few steps in the opposite direction before rewarding him. As he progresses, you'll be able to just give the verbal command, and he should still readily walk away from the distraction.

Advanced Commands

Some Greyhounds may not be interested in learning more advanced obedience skills, but you can always try teaching him things like tricks or agility. If you plan on competing in any dog sports, you can introduce sport-specific commands. The American Kennel Club has also introduced a Trick Dog title program, where your dog can earn titles just for performing his favorite tricks. There are five titles to be earned, each more challenging than the last.

If you'd prefer, you can also just increase the challenge of the commands your Greyhound already knows. Increase the duration of your stays, the distance of your recalls, or practice with more distractions.

No matter what you teach your Greyhound, just remember not to overdo it. Greyhounds are intelligent, but they aren't always interested in doing what they're told. By keeping your sessions short and interesting, you're more likely to keep your dog engaged rather than interested in what's happening in the next room. Pushing your dog past the limit of his attention span will only frustrate him and discourage him from wanting to learn more.

If your Greyhound seems to struggle with a certain command or skill, go back to something he's good at for a few repetitions so that you can reward him for doing something well and end on a good note. You can then return to the more difficult task in a later session when he's mentally rested and ready to learn once more.

CHAPTER 14
Nutrition

The Importance of a Balanced Diet

A balanced diet is essential to the health of Greyhounds of any age. If a dog is fed a diet lacking in nutrients, he may be at risk of developing serious health problems. This is especially true for growing puppies, whose development relies on a balanced diet. Puppies fed a subpar diet may suffer stunted growth or incorrect development. Unfortunately, diet imbalances are not immediately visible, and it can take weeks or even months before the effects of a poor diet can be seen. Not all effects of a poor diet can be fixed, and many dogs will have permanent health problems.

Photo Courtesy of Kennedy Vance

In addition to a proper balance of nutrients, portion size is also an essential part of feeding your Greyhound correctly. Obesity is one of the most common health issues in dogs of all breeds, and it can seriously impact your Greyhound's health no matter his age. Excess weight can cause serious strain on your Greyhound's joints, especially for growing puppies and aging seniors. Unfortunately, there is no precise guideline on how much food to give your dog each day. Different foods contain different amounts of calories. Growing puppies and active dogs will generally require more food than sedentary or senior dogs.

Basic Nutrition

Canine nutrition is not a simple subject, and many professionals, such as veterinary nutritionists, have dedicated their entire careers to understanding this complex topic. This book will cover only the basics of nutrition, so if you have any questions about this topic that aren't covered here, it's best to consult your veterinarian or a professional canine nutritionist.

Proteins and Amino Acids

Though you might have learned about the relationship between proteins and amino acids in school, few people retain that information well enough to consider them in the context of their Greyhound's diet. As you may recall, during digestion, proteins in food are broken down by the body into amino acids. These amino acids then combine to make different protein molecules that can be used by the body to grow, maintain, and repair cells. If you look at your Greyhound's current diet, you may notice that it has a higher protein content than you might expect. It's estimated that about 30 percent of your Greyhound's protein intake each day is used to maintain just the cells in his coat. The remaining 70 percent are used throughout your dog's body to build and maintain his skin, muscles, tendons, ligaments, and cartilage. Protein also influences your Greyhound's hormone production.

Your Greyhound's body requires 20 amino acids to form the various proteins needed for cell growth, maintenance, and repair. Some can be produced within the body, while others need to be supplied by your dog's food. The amino acids that cannot be produced by the body and must be supplied by food instead are referred to as essential amino acids. As the name suggests, these amino acids are essential to your dog's health, so it's crucial that his food provide them.

The ten essential amino acids are:

- Arginine
- Histidine
- Isoleucine
- Leucine
- Lysine
- Methionine
- Phenylalanine
- Threonine
- Tryptophan
- Valine

Protein and amino acids are often found in foods such as muscle meat, dairy products, and eggs. Though plants do contain some protein, it's generally not enough for your dog's body to thrive, so most balanced foods should contain more animal-based ingredients and fewer plant-based ingredients. Though some plant material is acceptable in a dog's diet, vegetarian and vegan diets are not biologically appropriate and should be avoided.

Fat and Fatty Acids

Fat is considered to be the most concentrated energy source for dogs and provides your Greyhound with fatty acids and calories. Calories are simply a unit to measure energy by, but fatty acids are organic materials necessary for cell growth and maintenance. Though similar to amino acids, fewer are required in a truly balanced diet. Many vitamins, such as A, D, E, and K, are fat-soluble, which means they can only be absorbed by the body once broken down by fat. Diets higher in fat are also generally more palatable for dogs, but caution must be taken as too much fat can have a negative impact on the dog's weight and overall health.

The essential fatty acids are:

- Arachidonic acid
- Linoleic acid
- Linolenic acid

You may have seen various treats, foods, and supplements promoting the benefits of omega-3 and omega-6 fatty acids. These fatty acids are necessary to a dog's well-being and are best consumed in a ratio of 4:1 with more omega-6s than omega-3s. Omega-3 fatty acids are provided by linolenic acid, while omega-6 fatty acids are provided by linoleic acid. Though you may also see omega-9 fatty acids in supplements marketed towards humans, omega-9s are of no use to the canine body and can actually decrease the concentration of omega-3s and -6s within the body.

Carbohydrates

Within the canine nutrition community, carbohydrates are a controversial topic. Though they do provide dogs with a source of energy, carbohydrates are generally not the most nutrient-dense or digestible food source. In fact, most carbohydrates can be excluded from a dog's diet with no ill effects. Many raw feeders opt to entirely exclude grain and carbohydrate-heavy vegetables from their dog's diet. Most commercially produced diets, such as kibble, use carbohydrates as a filler to help bring down the cost of the product to both the manufacturer and consumer. Owners who choose to feed their dogs homemade diets may choose the quantity of carbs in their dogs' diet, so long as it's still nutritionally balanced.

Carbohydrates are converted to usable energy once they are broken down by the digestive system into glucose. Many vegetables can also be a great source of antioxidants, phytochemicals, and minerals, as well as dietary fiber. However, it should be noted that many carbohydrates, especially starchy vegetables, will need to be cooked or pureed in order for them to be fully digestible by your Greyhound.

Feeding Puppies vs. Adult Dogs

Your Greyhound's nutritional needs are bound to change throughout his life, so it's important to adjust his diet on occasion to suit his changing body. Feeding a young puppy is not the same as feeding an active adult or senior Greyhound. When shopping for your dog's food, you may have noticed that there are different types of dog food marketed for dogs of different ages or life stages. Some food is labeled for "all life stages," which means that the food has met the Association of American Feed Control Officials' (AAFCO) standards for nutritional balance for dogs of any age. You will also notice foods labeled for use with puppies or seniors.

Choosing the right food requires you to evaluate your Greyhound's age and lifestyle and determine which type of food might work best. A growing Greyhound puppy requires a specific balance of nutrients in order for the dog to develop properly as it grows. Puppies also require a higher number of calories each day than the average adult dog. Once your Greyhound reaches adulthood, his dietary needs will vary according to his lifestyle. A relatively sedentary adult dog may eat a maintenance formula or a low-calorie formula, while an active adult dog may need larger portions or a high-performance formula.

As your Greyhound reaches his golden years, it's likely his physical activity and caloric intake will be far less than when he was younger. Greyhounds that have not been spayed or neutered will also require more calories than dogs that have been altered. Pregnant and lactating Greyhounds will also require a specific diet to keep them healthy as their puppies develop.

If you have multiple dogs in your home, consider buying different foods for each dog based on age and lifestyle to ensure that each dog is getting the nutrients it needs to thrive.

Different Types of Commercial Food

The most popular type of commercial dog food is kibble. Most owners choose to feed kibble because it's readily available, budget-friendly, and easy to feed. It's also available in a wide range of formulas to suit dogs of all ages, as well as those with medical issues or food sensitivities. Some kibble varieties are grain-free. You can also find kibble in a range of different protein options, including chicken, beef, and lamb, as well as novel proteins such as kangaroo, venison, and salmon. Kibble formulated for dogs with health issues may be available by prescription and can be more expensive than most kibble found at your local pet store.

For many dogs with food sensitivities, carbs such as corn, wheat, and soy are often to blame. For this reason, some owners choose to feed their dogs grain-free kibble, which contains different starchy vegetables such as peas or potatoes. However, it's important to note that some veterinarians advise against feeding grain-free diets due to the potential link between it and a heart disease called dilated cardiomyopathy, or DCM. Though the correlation is still being researched and the connection has not yet been confirmed, some vets prefer to reduce the risk by feeding dogs a diet containing grains.

Canned dog food is another popular choice for owners looking for a commercially available diet for their Greyhound. Canned food is much softer than kibble and tends to be more palatable, so it's ideal for picky eaters or Greyhounds that need to gain some weight. Canned food also contains more moisture than kibble, so it can be beneficial for dogs who tend not to drink enough water. As with kibble, you can find a range of different canned formulas to suit your dog's individual needs. Canned food does have a few downsides, but as long as you're paying attention to your dog's diet and health, you don't need to worry. Canned food can be more calorie-dense than many brands of kibble, so it's important to watch your dog's portion sizes. It also tends to stick to teeth more than kibble, so your Greyhound may need more frequent dental cleanings or teeth brushing.

Another increasingly popular choice is fresh-cooked dog food. Fresh-cooked dog food can be found in the refrigerated section of your local pet store or through online companies that send it straight to your doorstep. This type of food is frequently packaged in a roll and can be fed by simply slicing off a portion and returning the roll to the fridge. This type of food is often a great compromise for owners who want to give their Greyhound a fresher diet but without the effort of a homemade diet.

More Greyhound owners are also discovering the benefits of a biologically appropriate diet and are turning to the convenience of commercial raw diets. This type of food is made from a nutritionally balanced blend of meat, bones, and organs, as well as fruits and vegetables. Raw meals typically contain little to no grain, and once thawed, they have a consistency similar to fresh-cooked or some canned food. Commercial raw diets are designed to make meal prep and balance easy for any owner while still providing their dogs with the benefits of a raw diet.

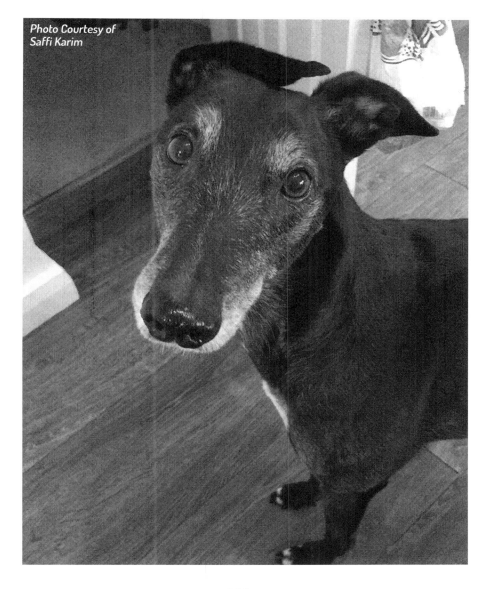

Photo Courtesy of
Saffi Karim

Commercial raw food is typically found in the freezer section of your local pet store. Like other foods, it's available in a range of proteins and serving sizes. This type of food is frequently frozen in ready-to-thaw pellets, medium-sized nuggets, or larger patties to accommodate dogs of all sizes and chewing abilities. Raw tends to be the most expensive commercial diet for dogs.

Homemade Diets

If you would like to be in full control of your Greyhound's nutrition, a homemade diet may be the right choice. Before you start, it's crucial to note that making your dog's food often requires a significant time commitment and can sometimes be more expensive than a commercially available diet. Additionally, commercial dog food is required by law to meet certain nutritional standards, so if you plan on making your Greyhound's food, it's up to you to make sure it's nutritionally balanced. Remember, nutritional imbalances are not always immediately apparent, so if your dog's homemade diet is lacking, you may not notice until the damage to his health has been done.

To help mitigate the risk of feeding your Greyhound a nutritionally imbalanced homemade diet, you should seek the guidance of a certified canine nutritionist. If you need help locating one, the American College of Veterinary Nutrition (ACVN) has a list of board-certified veterinary nutritionists on its website. It's worth noting that while some nutritionists follow AAFCO standards, many choose to follow the more stringent guidelines of the National Research Council (NRC). A canine nutritionist will be able to evaluate your dog's age, health, and lifestyle to formulate a healthy, balanced diet that you can make at home.

Raw diets are the most common homemade diet for dogs and typically fall into one of two categories: Biologically Appropriate Raw Food (BARF) or Prey Model Raw (PMR). PMR diets, or ratio diets, follow the approximate percentages of meat, bone, and organ in a prey animal. This type of diet is meant to simulate the diet of a wild dog. The most common formula to follow is 80% muscle meat, 10% bone, 10% liver, and 10% other secreting organs. With a PMR diet, fruits and vegetables are optional. Some owners feed a small amount, while others forgo all plant material.

BARF diets are similar and may follow a specified ratio, but there are generally more vegetables than in a PMR diet, including starchy vegetables and grains such as potato, oats, barley, or rice. Regardless of the type of diet, many raw feeders also supplement their dogs' diets with nutrient-packed additives like raw goat's milk, bone broth, or fermented fish stock. Whether you choose PMR or BARF, you should be aware that most raw diets based on percentages or ratios are lacking in certain nutrients like zinc, vitamin E, and manganese. Therefore, most raw feeders recommend working with a canine nutritionist.

Cooked diets are another option for owners who want to have full control over their Greyhound's diet but without the risks associated with raw diets. While there are some dogs who prefer cooked over raw, working with raw meat may be a risk for any immunocompromised people in the household. Many of the ingredients in a cooked diet are the same as in a raw diet, just baked or boiled before serving. Cooked diets also frequently contain more carbs, such as barley, rice, or oats.

The only big difference between ingredients in a raw and cooked diet is the lack of bones. Calcium is typically provided with the addition of ground eggshells, seaweed calcium, or another calcium supplement. Cooked bones (as opposed to raw) should not be fed to any dog due to the risk of splintering.

If you choose to supplement your Greyhound's homemade diet with raw bones, it's important to use caution. Weight-bearing bones, such as those from the legs of large animals like cattle, are incredibly dense and can potentially cause your dog to break or chip a tooth. Additionally, marrow bones can get caught on the jaw in a way that may hurt your dog or cause him to panic. Heavy chewers should only be given softer bones to chew on, or the bone should be taken away after the dog has chewed the meat off.

Always supervise your Greyhound any time you feed him raw bones so that you can assist or stop him if necessary. Not all dogs will understand that they need to chew large chunks of food, and they may try to gulp it down in one go. Some dogs may learn with experience, while others will never stop gulping. For these types of dogs, grinding their food is recommended or feeding them chunks of food large enough that they won't attempt to swallow it whole.

If you choose to feed your Greyhound a homemade diet, it's important that you consider all risks involved. This includes keeping your human family members safe. When proper hygiene practices are followed, very few raw feeders experience illnesses such as salmonella. Whether you're feeding your Greyhound raw meat or preparing to cook it for him, you need to clean your prep area appropriately. It's also recommended to restrict your dog's access to the house while he's eating. Some dogs take their food to another area to eat, which can be a problem if they're spreading potentially dangerous pathogens around your home.

Do not allow your Greyhound to consume raw meat on carpet or furniture as these surfaces can be difficult to clean properly. Instead, consider feeding him outside if the weather permits or in his kennel or playpen. You might also consider wiping down your Greyhound's paws and face after each meal to further prevent the spread of germs.

Weight Management

According to a study performed by the Association of Pet Obesity Prevention, approximately 52% of adult dogs are overweight or obese, but 90% of owners do not recognize that their dogs are above a healthy weight. Obesity is a serious problem that can affect your Greyhound's health and happiness. While you should monitor your Greyhound's weight, your veterinarian is also a great resource for proper weight management.

According to the AKC's breed standard, Greyhounds should weigh between 60 and 70 pounds. However, this doesn't mean that if your dog is within this range that he's a healthy weight. Though the breed standard is a helpful guide, it's not accurate in evaluating your dog's healthiest weight. A particularly small Greyhound with a small frame may weigh closer to 50 pounds. A more average-sized Greyhound may do better at 60 pounds rather than 70 pounds.

It's also important to realize that sighthounds, such as the Greyhound, tend to have far less body fat than other breeds. Sighthounds tend to have a leaner appearance, which can cause uninformed people to believe that the dog is underweight. While other breeds may be healthiest with a layer of fat over their ribs, if the ribs of a Greyhound are not visible, it's likely that the dog is overweight.

Portion size is by far the most important aspect of proper weight management. Just don't forget to include your Greyhound's daily allotment of training treats and chews into your calculations. It can be easy to focus on the size of your dog's breakfast and dinner while forgetting that he also gets additional calories throughout the day. If your Greyhound needs to cut back, you might also consider swapping high-calorie training treats for healthier options like vegetables or a portion of his breakfast or dinner. You may also use fruit but use caution as it is high in sugar.

The other important factor to consider in managing your Greyhound's weight is the amount of physical activity he receives each day. The more active your dog is, the more food he's going to be able to eat without it affecting his waistline. If your Greyhound needs to lose a few pounds, it can be helpful to slowly increase his physical activity while also limiting his portion sizes. As long as your dog doesn't have any mobility issues, physical exercise is also a great way to keep him busy and out of trouble.

Food Allergies and Intolerances

Food allergies are one of the five most common allergies or hypersensitivities for dogs of all breeds, and Greyhounds are no exception. Food allergies are caused by an overreaction of your Greyhound's immune system in response to certain proteins in his diet. These reactions are typically referred to as either allergies or intolerances, depending on the severity. For some dogs, the immune system's reaction may include digestive upset or generalized itching. Other dogs may experience more severe symptoms like ear and skin infections, vomiting, and diarrhea. Though any ingredient can cause a reaction, some of the most common allergens include beef, chicken, corn, lamb, soy, and wheat.

Unfortunately, the diagnosis of food allergies or intolerances is not a simple process. In many cases, owners will need to work with their vets for months, narrowing down the suspected problem ingredient. To do this, most vets recommend an elimination diet. Elimination diets can take several weeks or months to complete, but with any luck, you should be able to figure out what ingredient is causing your Greyhound's reaction.

While on an elimination diet, dogs are placed on a type of food formulated with a novel protein such as venison, salmon, or kangaroo. Novel proteins are less likely to cause a reaction, so they're generally the best place to start. If possible, choose a food with limited ingredients to help reduce the likelihood of a reaction at first. After feeding this food for a few weeks, you can determine whether you believe your dog is doing well. If so, you can introduce another more common protein and feed that for a few weeks. If there is no reaction, you can move on to the next. Each protein will need to be fed for at least a few weeks to ensure there is enough time for the dog's immune system to react if it's going to.

In some cases, a dog's immune system may overreact to any number of proteins, making it difficult to narrow down the culprit. If this is the case with your Greyhound, your vet may recommend a hypoallergenic diet. The food in these diets is made from hydrolyzed proteins, which are broken down into small particles so as to bypass the immune system. Hypoallergenic diets are usually only available by prescription, so you may need to purchase the food from your vet. Unless money is of no concern, hypoallergenic diets are often a last resort, as they can be quite expensive.

Sighthound Nutrition

As mentioned previously, what you feed your Greyhound, as well as how much, will depend on your dog's age and lifestyle. Regardless of what you feed your dog, you may notice that he occasionally goes off his feed. This is not unusual for Greyhounds, as they can be finicky eaters, especially in times of stress. In most cases, it's not harmful for a dog to miss a meal or two. However, not eating can also be a symptom of bloat, so you'll need to watch your Greyhound carefully to make sure you're able to tell the difference between the dog being picky and needing to see a vet.

Sighthounds are deep-chested breeds, which can put them at a higher risk of bloat (this is discussed in more detail later in the book). This is especially true if your Greyhound tends to gulp his food down along with some air. To minimize the risk of bloat, it's recommended to keep your dog relatively calm before and after mealtimes. This doesn't mean he needs to be crated, but you should not allow him to race around the yard or wrestle wildly with your other dogs. It's recommended to limit strenuous exercise two hours before and two hours after eating. For some dogs, drinking an excessive amount of water may also lead to bloat, so it's best to interrupt your Greyhound if he tends to gulp large amounts of water at mealtime. It's also advisable to feed your sighthound smaller amounts multiple times per day, rather than one big meal. Feeding two or three meals per day is best, depending on your schedule and your Greyhound's preferences.

If your Greyhound has recently retired from the track, you might consider allowing him to gain a bit of weight. Greyhounds should never be

FUN FACT
Racing Greyhounds' Diet

Racing Greyhounds' diets vary from trainer to trainer, so while it's impossible to point to an official dietary regimen for these athletic dogs, it's safe to say that racing Greyhounds require a high protein diet for optimal speed. Up to 70 percent of this protein often comes from raw meat, which is believed to supply the dogs with more vitamins and minerals than cooked meat. Unfortunately, raw meat can also expose dogs to food-borne pathogens such as salmonella and E. coli. The Texas Greyhound Association feeds its dogs a light protein meal before racing and a regular full meal once the dogs have cooled down on race days. Retired racing Greyhounds should have a diet composed of no more than 30 percent protein. Nutritional needs can vary from dog to dog, so be sure to check with your veterinarian when establishing a new dietary routine for your Greyhound.

allowed to become overweight, but a sighthound at racing weight is thinner than one at a healthy pet weight. Remember, your dog was previously working as a professional athlete, so it's to be expected that his body will change once he goes from peak physical fitness to a more relaxed lifestyle. Many rescue staff members recommend allowing your rescued Greyhound to gain about five pounds above his racing weight. This number will vary according to your dog's individual build, but it's a general guideline you may follow if you wish.

CHAPTER 15
Physical and Mental Exercise

The Importance of Physical Exercise

Physical exercise is essential to the well-being of any Greyhound. When combined with feeding appropriately sized portions, physical exercise will help keep your Greyhound at a healthy weight. Obesity is one of the most common health issues among adult dogs of all breeds, and affected dogs are

Photo Courtesy of
Susie Morris

at higher risk of developing related issues such as diabetes, heart disease, and arthritis. The more obese a dog is, the more painful it will be to move, which will further limit his mobility. This can make losing weight incredibly difficult, so it's generally best to prevent excess weight gain rather than try to get an overweight dog to lose weight.

Additionally, physical exercise is key in preventing the development of bad behaviors. A tired Greyhound is far less likely to engage in destructive behaviors than a bored Greyhound with pent-up energy. This can be more challenging with dogs with mobility issues, but exercise does not have to be solely physical to provide benefits.

The exact amount of exercise needed by your Greyhound each day will vary according to his individual needs. Your dog's age, health, and energy level will all need to be considered. Some Greyhounds may be fine with a long walk and short training session each day, while others may need more. It's also important to note that puppies and seniors will not have the stamina of an adult Greyhound and will not be able to exercise for such long periods. Greyhounds with health or mobility issues will also require different care than healthy adult dogs. In general, it's recommended you provide your Greyhound with at least an hour of physical and mental activity each day. However, if your dog has any health problems, it's best to consult your veterinarian before starting any exercise program.

It's worth noting that you do not need to dedicate an entire block of time to exercising your Greyhound each day. The amount of time you spend exercising your dog can and should be broken down into shorter sessions throughout the day. For example, if you plan to exercise your Greyhound for an hour each day, you can do 30 minutes before you leave for work and another 30 minutes when you return home in the evening. Training sessions should be kept even shorter, and you can sprinkle these throughout your day as you see fit. This is especially true for young and old dogs that can't work for long periods of time. However, if you have a Greyhound that tends to get anxious when left alone, it's generally recommended to exercise him for as long as possible before you leave for work. That way, he'll be tired enough that he's more likely to spend the day sleeping rather than fretting about being alone.

You should also consider mixing up your activities to ensure that you and your Greyhound stay engaged and enthusiastic about your exercise. If you can take your Greyhound for a hike some days or attend training sessions, your Greyhound will not only benefit from that socialization, but he'll be able to exercise his mind as well as his body. Even taking different routes on your walks will be enough to keep things interesting for both of you.

Exercising Puppies

If you have a young Greyhound, you'll need to be especially careful when exercising him to ensure that you don't accidentally damage his developing body. Most veterinarians recommend using caution when exercising dogs under the age of about 18 months as their growth plates have not yet fused. Of course, this doesn't mean you need to avoid strenuous exercise altogether, but you just need to be careful not to overstress your dog's growing body. Low-impact exercises are generally recommended over activities such as agility that can expose your puppy's joints to the impacts of jumping.

If your daily activities are more mental than physical, you'll also need to use some restraint. Puppies do not have the attention spans of adult Greyhounds, so it's best to keep training sessions short. Training sessions can be repeated throughout the day as needed, but it's generally recommended to quit before your puppy loses interest. This can vary from puppy to puppy, but if you notice your puppy becoming less engaged at around seven minutes into your training session, consider quitting after just five minutes. If you continually work your puppy to the point of exhaustion or frustration, he'll begin to associate these problems with working with you, and he will be less engaged in future sessions. If he seems to be struggling in a particular session, you might want to keep the session even shorter than usual.

There is some debate on how much exercise is too much exercise for a puppy. Some socialization and training programs, like Puppy Culture,

Photo Courtesy of Nicole Becker

Photo Courtesy of Savannah Peeples

recommend no more than five minutes for every month of a puppy's age. This means that a six-month-old puppy should not be exercised more than 30 minutes per day. For some puppies, this may be appropriate, but high-energy or high-drive Greyhounds may need more exercise to ensure that their needs are met each day.

For a more precise recommendation, it's best to ask your veterinarian, who will be able to make a recommendation based on your Greyhound's health and fitness rather than a general guideline. In many cases, you may be able to rely on your puppy to set his own boundaries. Greyhounds do not generally have the endless energy of some other working breeds, so they often let you know when they're done.

Exercising Former Racing Dogs

In most cases, a former racer will be able to handle the same amount of exercise as any other Greyhound of the same age. Ex-racers often come off the track in peak physical condition, but it's still best to start slow if you're expecting any type of endurance out of your new dog. Remember, Greyhounds are sprinters, so they're used to running as fast as they can for short distances and may not have the fitness for a long hike, for example.

If your Greyhound experienced any injuries during his time at the track, you'll also need to consider this when determining how much to exercise your new dog. Most injured dogs will require a rehab period, and you may need to discuss your Greyhound's condition with a veterinarian specializing in sports rehabilitation. As always, if you have any questions or concerns about your ex-racer's fitness, consult your veterinarian.

The Importance of Mental Exercise

Though Greyhounds are prized for their physical athleticism, it's important not to overlook their mental needs as well. Though Greyhounds have a reputation for being wonderful house dogs, an understimulated Greyhound can easily destroy your home or possessions. As the owner of a Greyhound, if you have any mobility issues, you'll also need to find ways to keep your dog busy without stressing your own body, and mental stimulation is a great way to accomplish this.

Mental stimulation comes in a variety of forms but typically requires your dog to think about his actions and behavior. Training sessions are a fun way to accomplish this while bonding with your dog and teaching him new commands. The American Kennel Club has a Trick Dog title program that can provide you with fun goals to teach your Greyhound new tricks. Or you can train for other dog sports or just for fun. Puzzle toys are also a fun way to get your Greyhound to use his mind while trying to get tasty treats out of a complicated toy.

Sports such as scentwork and barn hunt are another great way to get your Greyhound to use his nose and mind. These types of sports are ideal for dogs or owners with limited mobility as they require plenty of mental strength but not as much physical movement as more active dog sports like agility or rally.

Greyhounds and Dog Sports

As a naturally athletic breed, the Greyhound is built to excel in dog sports, especially sports designed specifically for sighthounds. Any sport involving the Greyhound's natural prey drive and desire to run would be the ideal place to start if you're new to dog sports in general. There are Greyhounds competing successfully in nearly every dog sport, but they are few and far between. In general, Greyhounds do not have any interest in sports where they need to maintain constant focus on the handler. If you desire to compete in these types of sports with your Greyhound, you'll need to keep this in mind while you search for the perfect dog. Not every Greyhound is suited for every type of sport, so you may need to look for an especially biddable individual if you want to compete in handler-oriented dog sports.

Lure Coursing

Photo Courtesy of Amy King

The most popular dog sport for Greyhounds, as well as other sighthounds, is lure coursing. Lure coursing is an exciting event that allows your dog to satisfy his need to chase down prey in a safe and controlled environment. For ex-racers, this sport is similar to the dog's experience on the track. Most lure coursing events are offered either by the American Kennel Club (AKC) or the American Sighthound Field Association (ASFA).

In most cases, a lure course measures between 500 and 1000 yards in length, though they can be longer on occasion. The lure itself is typically a piece of plastic, similar to a plastic bag, attached to a string. The continuous loop of braided string is stretched across the course, connected by a series of pulleys. The string is set up in a way that resembles the natural path of a fleeing prey animal, without any close, tight turns that could potentially cause injury. The string is then run through a wheel attached to a motor, which is controlled by a lure operator. The lure operator has complete control over the lure's movement, and an experienced operator is an expert at simulating the behavior of a prey animal.

Lure coursing is not an individual sport, so if your Greyhound is aggressive or nervous around other dogs, this is not the appropriate sport for him. Generally, sighthounds are run in groups of two or three dogs of the same breed, though sometimes groups may be larger. Dogs only compete against others of their breed because different sighthounds have different styles of running. For example, a Basenji and a Greyhound are both sighthounds, but running them together would not be fair as they are not the same size, nor

FUN FACT
Record High Jumps

On September 14, 2017, a Greyhound named Feather set the world record for highest jump by a dog. Her jump measured 75.5 in or 191.7 cm. Feather is a rescue dog from Frederick, Maryland, and was adopted and trained by Samantha Valle.

do they have the same running style. Additionally, some clubs have rules regarding muzzles. Many sighthounds run in muzzles for the safety of the other dogs, but some dogs will run just fine without them if it is permitted.

Lure coursing trials are observed by a qualified judge to ensure that the competition is fair for all involved, as well as to ensure the safety of the dogs competing. When your Greyhound competes in a lure coursing trial, he will be able to earn points during each run. The number of points earned will depend on how well he performs. With enough points, he will be able to earn titles. Titles are offered by both AKC and ASFA. Additionally, most clubs offer ribbons and rosettes to their competitors to celebrate their success.

If you're interested in getting started, the best way to learn more about lure coursing is to contact a local sighthound club. You may be able to attend a trial and see how the dogs are run and how the handlers prepare their dogs. Most people in the dog sport community are friendly and welcoming to new people, so feel free to ask questions. Just be sure you aren't trying to ask questions as people are getting their dogs ready to run, as they may not have time to accommodate your requests.

FastCAT

FastCAT is a competition offered by the AKC that is similar to lure coursing but less technical. FastCAT is short for Fast Coursing Ability Test. It is open to all breeds, so you'll see more than just sighthounds at a FastCAT test. Like lure coursing, a plastic lure is attached to a string, but rather than the long, complicated course you'd see at a lure coursing trial, FastCAT is a straight run of 100 yards. Most Greyhounds will be able to complete their run in well under 10 seconds. In FastCAT, dogs are run individually and are not required to wear muzzles or the colored blankets used in coursing. However, if your dog runs better in a muzzle, this is permitted.

Dogs competing in FastCAT are able to earn titles through the AKC. For Greyhounds and similarly sized dogs, the speed they run equals the number of points the dog receives for that individual run. Each run will have a different result, and your dog will earn a different number of points. The first FastCAT title is BCAT, which is earned when your dog accumulates 150 points. At 500 points, your dog earns the DCAT title, and at 1000 points, your dog can earn the FCAT title. For every 500 points beyond the FCAT title, a number will be added. For example, at 1500 points, the dog will earn the title FCAT1, and at 2000 points, the dog will reach FCAT2. Additionally, most clubs offering FastCAT tests will have ribbons and rosettes available for eligible dogs.

Other Dog Sports

As previously stated, not all Greyhounds are suitable for all types of dog sports. There are Greyhounds who do not enjoy chasing a lure. If you'd like to compete with your Greyhound, it can be helpful to try out a variety of sports to see what your dog might enjoy and excel at. Depending on where you live, you should be able to find dog sport clubs offering an array of training and competition opportunities.

Scentwork can be a great sport for Greyhounds who enjoy using their nose. It's especially fun for dogs with mobility problems that can no longer compete in more strenuous sports like lure coursing. In scentwork, dogs must search a designated area to locate a specific scent. Once found, the dog must alert the handler to the presence of the scent. As with other sports, a dog that successfully completes the task at hand will earn ribbons, rosettes, and titles.

Barn hunt is another sport that takes advantage of a dog's powerful sense of smell. This sport, in particular, also engages a dog's prey drive as the dogs must search for rats. The rats are protected in PVC tubes for their safety and hidden among bales of straw. Competing dogs must search the bales of straw for the correct tube. Empty tubes and tubes full of rat litter are also present, but the dog is required to ignore these. Again, ribbons, rosettes, and titles can be earned with enough qualifying runs.

If you're feeling ambitious with your Greyhound, you might want to try attending classes for other sports such as obedience, rally, or agility. These sports require more focus than most Greyhounds would prefer, but it can still be a fun way to bond with your dog and keep him busy. Don't be afraid to step out of your comfort zone to try something new. You might just find that your Greyhound loves it!

CHAPTER 16
Grooming

Coat Basics

When it comes to coat maintenance, the Greyhound is an incredibly easy breed to care for. Their sleek coat requires minimal care aside from occasional brushing and a bath when necessary. Greyhounds are average shedders and tend to shed year-round rather than seasonally. The exact amount of hair your Greyhound leaves around your home will depend on a few factors, including his diet. Generally, dogs on high-quality diets will shed less than dogs eating poor-quality food.

To help keep shedding to a minimum, brush your Greyhound a few times per week. Thankfully, this isn't time-consuming. Plus, most Greyhounds enjoy the massage, so brushing isn't usually a difficult task to complete.

Essential Grooming Tools

If you plan on grooming your Greyhound at home, you'll need to have a few grooming tools on hand. The tool you'll find yourself using most often is a brush, so it's important to choose one that's comfortable for you and your dog. For a short, sleek coat, a rubber curry brush is one of the most effective brushes. These can be used wet or dry to help remove dead hair and stimulate blood flow.

Some owners use a deshedding brush, but it's important to use this tool with caution. Greyhounds often have sensitive skin, and it's possible to accidentally scratch the skin or damage the coat if the deshedding brush is used incorrectly. Many Greyhounds have areas with particularly thin hair, such as the back of the thighs, so you'll need to be especially careful in those areas. If you're ever unsure of what brush works best or how to use it, consult your local groomer.

A high-quality shampoo and conditioner are also essential grooming items that you'll need if you don't want to take your Greyhound to a professional. Dog shampoos and conditioners are available in a wide range of scents and formulas, so you'll need to choose according to your dog's individual needs. Some dogs have sensitive skin and need a gentler formula, while others may get dirty so often that they need a stronger shampoo to control their odor. For dogs without issues, you might just need to choose the scent you like best.

Whatever you choose, look for a shampoo with plenty of natural ingredients. Shampoos containing numerous chemicals or artificial ingredients are more likely to irritate your dog's skin, so it's best to choose a natural product if possible. It's important to note that many natural products are low-sudsing, which means you'll see fewer bubbles in the bath. This doesn't mean the product isn't cleaning effectively.

Conditioners, if you choose to use them, are generally available in formulas that complement your shampoo of choice. Greyhounds with sensitive skin or a dry coat may need something soothing, but for dogs with a healthy coat, conditioner is entirely optional. Some conditioners can lengthen the coat's drying time, so you might consider using a leave-in conditioning spray if you need your dog to dry quickly.

If you choose to brush your Greyhound's teeth at home between professional cleanings, you'll also need to invest in a doggie toothbrush and toothpaste. There are many different styles of toothbrushes to choose from, but be sure to use only toothpaste formulated for dogs as human toothpaste can be toxic to dogs.

The final tool you'll need to groom your Greyhound at home is a high-quality nail trimmer or grinder. Whether you use clippers or a grinder is up to you, but many dogs find the grinder to be more tolerable than clippers. If you do choose clippers, look for scissor-style clippers rather than guillotine-style. Scissor-style clippers tend to make a cleaner cut with less crushing damage than guillotine-style clippers.

Grinders are the preferred option for many owners as they tend to be safer. Not only is the risk of cutting the nail too short reduced, but the sharp edges of a freshly clipped nail are eliminated. This will help prevent your dog from accidentally scratching you and your furniture. Nail grinders may be either corded or cordless, so you'll need to decide which you prefer. If you're unsure of the correct technique to trim your Greyhound's nails, consider asking your vet or groomer for advice.

Bathing

The frequency with which you bathe your Greyhound will depend on several things. If you live in an area where your dog has the freedom to get dirty often, and he enjoys doing so, you're going to need to bathe him more frequently than if you live in a city with a Greyhound that prefers to stay clean. Additionally, if your Greyhound has any skin issues, you may need to bathe him more or less frequently and possibly use special medicated shampoos. Most groomers recommend 8 to 12 weeks as a guideline because this frequency will keep your Greyhound's skin and coat in top condition, but you should always adjust this schedule to your Greyhound's individual needs. You don't want to wash him too frequently as this can dry out his coat and skin, potentially causing irritation. However, you need to bathe him often enough to prevent the buildup of dirt, oil, and dead hair, which can also cause skin irritation.

HELPFUL TIP
Oatmeal Bath

If your dog has sensitive skin, you might consider giving him an oatmeal bath. Oatmeal baths are soothing to the skin and easy to do! First, grind up some oats in a coffee grinder or food processor. Add the oats to your dog's bath and stir the water to distribute them. Allow your dog to soak if he'd like, then towel dry.

Unless you're using a medicated shampoo that requires direct application to the skin, it's generally recommended to wet your Greyhound before applying shampoo. A wet coat is easier to scrub and spread the shampoo throughout. Since the shampoo needs to make direct contact with the

skin in order to be effective, wetting the coat prior to applying shampoo can help it penetrate the top layer of the coat. If you've invested in a rubber curry brush, now is a great time to use it. The brush will not only help distribute the shampoo throughout the coat, but it will also help scrub away dead skin cells, hair, and dirt. Plus, your Greyhound will likely enjoy the massage.

It's crucial to always prioritize your Greyhound's comfort and safety during the bath. When shampooing, avoid getting any product in your dog's ears and eyes. It can be helpful to put cotton balls in your dog's ears before bathing, but you'll need to remember to take them out when you're finished. If you're worried about getting shampoo into your dog's eyes, you might consider having an eye rinse on hand or just using a wet washcloth to wipe down his face. If you're using a rubber curry brush, you'll also need to avoid delicate or bony areas. The brush should not be used to scrub your Greyhound's private parts, legs, tail, or face. These areas can be sensitive and are best washed by hand.

When you're done shampooing, you'll need to make sure all product is rinsed from your dog's coat. Shampoo residue can cause irritation and even hot spots, so it's crucial that the coat is rinsed thoroughly. The best method to ensure that the coat is clean is that when you're sure that you're done rinsing, you do it once more just to be sure. If you've chosen to follow up with a conditioner, you'll need to repeat the process.

Since Greyhounds do not have a thick coat, they can be dried with a towel. A good scrubbing with a towel can help remove the last bit of dead hair, and your Greyhound may enjoy the feeling. However, many dogs get the post-bath "zoomies," and you may not want your damp dog racing through your home. If this is the case, you can use either a handheld dryer or a high-velocity dryer like the professionals use. High-velocity dryers can dry a Greyhound's coat in a matter of minutes, but they can be expensive. Use whatever drying method you feel is best for your Greyhound.

Brushing

Even though Greyhounds' coats are low-maintenance, they are not "no maintenance." Brushing your Greyhound's coat a few times per week will help keep his skin and coat in top condition while also limiting the amount of hair he leaves around your home. Greyhounds certainly do not shed as much as other breeds, but they do shed consistently year-round. Not all dogs enjoy brushing at first, but with patience and plenty of praise, your Greyhound will come to enjoy this one-on-one time with you.

As previously mentioned, a rubber curry brush is the best tool for grooming a Greyhound. However, you must be careful to use the right amount of pressure to be effective without hurting your dog. You need to use enough pressure to thoroughly remove dirt, hair, and dander but not so much that you cause discomfort or pain. Again, you'll need to be careful to avoid sensitive areas such as the privates, legs, tail, and face. If you're still not sure how best to use your brush, ask your local groomer for a demonstration at your Greyhound's next grooming appointment.

Cleaning Eyes and Ears

While most Greyhound owners keep up with their dog's coat and nail maintenance, the eyes and ears are often overlooked. Though Greyhounds are not particularly prone to problems in these areas, checking them periodically can help keep any potential infections or irritation at bay. You'll need to be sure to clean your Greyhound's ears after any exposure to moisture, such as during a bath or swimming. When moisture is trapped inside the ears, the moisture and your dog's natural body heat create the perfect environment for yeast and bacteria to thrive.

If you notice your Greyhound scratching at one or both ears or rubbing his head on the floor, he may have an infection. If you look inside his ear, you may also notice redness or swelling. An unpleasant odor emanating

*Photo Courtesy of
Savannah Peeples*

from the ear is also a common symptom of an ear infection. If you notice any of these symptoms, take your Greyhound to the vet as soon as possible. The infection may be caused by either yeast or bacteria, which require different treatments.

To clean your Greyhound's ears, you need to first purchase an ear cleaner. There are two types of ear cleaner to choose from: alcohol-based or non-alcohol. Alcohol-based cleaners evaporate quickly and are ideal for drying out an ear after exposure to water. However, if there is an infection present or your dog is sensitive, alcohol can cause an unpleasant sensation. If this is the case, a non-alcohol cleaner is recommended. It's also recommended to use cotton balls over cotton swabs as there is less of a risk of accidentally injuring your Greyhound's ears. Cotton swabs can reach deep into the ear canal, potentially damaging delicate structures. Using a cotton ball with your fingers is unlikely to cause any injury.

To clean your Greyhound's ears, wet a cotton ball thoroughly with cleaner and squeeze out the excess. Insert the cotton ball into the ear and gently wipe away the inside of the ear leather as well as the ear canal. Your finger is too large to reach any delicate structures, so if you are gentle, your Greyhound shouldn't protest. However, if he has an infection, his ears may be painful, and he may not tolerate rough handling of his ears. After all visible dirt and grime has been wiped away, you can wipe the ear with a dry cotton ball to help absorb the excess cleaner and prevent your Greyhound from shaking it all over your home.

Few Greyhounds have problems with tear staining, so you likely won't need to clean your dog's eyes often. It's not uncommon for dogs to have a bit of crusty discharge at the corners of their eyes that can be wiped off using a soft cloth. If you would prefer, you can also use a damp cloth or pre-soaked eye wipes. Whenever you clean around your Greyhound's eyes, just be careful that you do not accidentally scratch or poke him in the eye. Additionally, if you notice a sudden increase or change in your Greyhound's eye discharge, it may be best to consult your veterinarian. Sudden changes can indicate a problem, and it's best to address it sooner rather than later.

Trimming Nails

Whether you plan to do it at home or have a professional groomer take care of it, your Greyhound's nails will need to be trimmed on a regular basis. Nails that are not trimmed on a regular basis will grow long enough to affect your Greyhound's gait and musculoskeletal structure. This is especially true if your Greyhound is young and still growing.

How often you trim your Greyhound's nails will depend on a few factors. If you frequently walk your dog on pavement, his nails may wear down naturally and need trimming less frequently than a dog who is walked on soft dirt or grass. Some dogs' nails also just grow more quickly than others. Owners that like to stay on top of their Greyhound's nails may choose to trim them as often as once per week, while others may choose to do it on a monthly basis. As long as you don't let your Greyhound's nails grow long enough to affect his movement, you can choose a schedule that works for you.

Before you trim your Greyhound's nails, you'll need to locate the quick. The quick is the nail's blood supply, and if it's trimmed too short, you risk injuring your dog. If your Greyhound has light-colored nails, the quick will be easy to locate, but it can be more difficult on dark-colored nails. For dark-colored nails you'll need to trim in thin layers rather than taking off a large chunk of nail at once.

As you trim away layers, look for a dark circle in the center of the nail. That is the quick, and if you keep trimming once you see it, you'll "quick" your dog, and the nail will bleed profusely. Even professional groomers have been known to quick a dog on occasion, so you may want to have styptic powder on hand to control the bleeding. This process of locating the quick and trimming in layers will need to be repeated for each nail. If your Greyhound has dewclaws, don't forget to trim them, too, since they don't experience the same rate of wear as the other nails.

HELPFUL TIP
Racers' Paws

If you're adopting a retired racing Greyhound, your dog's paw pads and toenails could be in rough shape from years of racing. You can pamper your pup's feet if they look cracked or dry. Avoid using moisturizers intended for human use, and look for products tailored for your canine companion. Regular nail maintenance and paw checks are an essential part of your dog's paw health, so be sure to make this part of your grooming routine.

If your Greyhound is patient and docile, nail trims can take just a few minutes. However, if your dog is less tolerant, or you simply don't want to trim his nails yourself, make an appointment with your vet or groomer. Nail trims are typically inexpensive and often cost less than $20. Not all facilities require appointments for nail trims, but it's best to call and ask. Don't forget to tip your groomer for his or her hard work!

Even if your Greyhound is a bit difficult to handle for nail trims, a few professional sessions may be enough to give him confidence, and he should settle down. If you want to take over the job yourself, you can also ask your groomer for advice on handling and trimming techniques.

Brushing Your Dog's Teeth

All dogs will require professional dental cleanings at some point in their lives, but professional cleanings may be done less frequently if you're willing to maintain your Greyhound's dental health at home. If you're on the fence about whether this is necessary, consider what your own teeth might look like if you only relied on your annual visits to the dentist.

Even if you don't plan on brushing your dog's teeth each day, you'll still need to check them regularly to make sure there are no problems. Depending on your Greyhound's diet, tartar and plaque may develop quickly, and periodontal disease may develop before you know it. The bacteria present in plaque and tartar can easily enter the bloodstream and spread throughout your dog's body, potentially causing serious illness. If dental problems are left unchecked, tooth loss is also a common occurrence. Thankfully, all of these problems are preventable with regular veterinary checkups and consistent at-home care.

If you don't yet have a toothbrush and toothpaste for your Greyhound, you'll need to purchase them. Doggie toothbrushes are available in a range of styles, but the most popular ones either slip over your finger or resemble a human toothbrush. No style is better than any other, so choose what works best for you. Children's toothbrushes are often the right size and softness for dogs as well. However, you will need to buy a toothpaste specifically formulated for dogs. Human toothpastes contain ingredients that are unsafe for dogs. If you'd prefer not to buy doggie toothpaste or have trouble finding it at your local pet store, you can also make a paste out of baking soda and water.

Before you dive into brushing your Greyhound's teeth, you'll need to get him used to the idea of having things in his mouth. If you've purchased flavored doggie toothpaste, you can try putting a bit of paste on your finger and having him lick it off. Then you can progress to having him lick it off his toothbrush. As he adjusts, you can try lifting his lips up and eventually work your way toward scrubbing a few teeth. Try not to brush too vigorously, especially at first, as you may make your dog uncomfortable and cause him to resist. Don't forget to tell your Greyhound how good he is. Plenty of praise and affection will encourage him to sit quietly the next time.

Even if you brush your Greyhound's teeth each and every day, you'll still need to have your vet perform regular dental cleanings. Most vets recommend checkups once or twice per year, but the frequency will depend on your Greyhound's age and overall health. Your veterinarian will be able to give you a more accurate suggestion on how often you should bring your dog in. It's important to note that your dog will need to undergo anesthesia in order to thoroughly and safely clean his teeth. This procedure is incredibly safe, but if you have any questions, be sure to ask before you drop your dog off for his cleaning.

When Professional Help is Necessary

Since Greyhounds are so easy to groom, many owners feel guilty about asking someone else to take care of it, but there is no shame in asking for help. Greyhounds are large dogs, and not everyone is able or willing to groom them at home. For many people, it's far easier just to drop their dogs off for a spa appointment than to wrestle them into the bath at home. Many dogs come to love their time with their groomer and see them as a new friend. As long as you remember to include grooming costs in your monthly budget, there's no reason that you should have to groom your Greyhound at home if you don't want to.

CHAPTER 17
Basic Health Care

Visiting the Vet

After you bring your Greyhound home, visiting the vet will become a regular event in your life. Depending on your Greyhound's health and age, you'll need to take him to the vet at least as often as every six to twelve months. If your Greyhound is in good health, this may seem unnecessary, but regular checkups are crucial in catching problems before they can seriously affect your dog's health. It's not uncommon for health problems to progress more quickly than you'd expect, so it's important to catch them in the early stages and treat them as quickly as possible.

HELPFUL TIP
Greyhound Health Research

Did you know that the Greyhound Club of America (GCA) helps to fund research projects through the American Kennel Club Health Foundation? As of April 2015, the GCA has donated over $160,000 to the cause. Research programs that have been supported include epilepsy research, genome analyses, thyroid research, and many others. For a complete list of research programs that have been partially funded by the GCA, visit www.greyhoundclubofamerica. org/research-articles/

While you can monitor your Greyhound at home for abnormal occurrences, only your vet will be able to test your dog for dangerous internal parasites such as heartworm. Additionally, when you see your dog every day, it can be difficult to notice some changes, such as weight gain, whereas your vet will be able to compare with the notes from your dog's last visit. This can make subtle changes in your Greyhound's condition more obvious. If you're unsure of how frequently you need to schedule checkups for your Greyhound, ask your veterinarian.

Allergies

One of the most common health problems in dogs of all breeds is allergies. Allergies rarely appear in dogs under six months of age, and most do not receive a diagnosis until after one or two years of age. The exact reason that some dogs develop allergies is unknown. Some experts believe there may be a genetic cause, but whatever the reason, it's clear that most allergies are due to a hypersensitive immune system. Though dogs can be allergic to any potential allergen in their environment, the most common causes are food, plants, insects, and other animals.

If your Greyhound has allergies, his exact symptoms will depend on the allergen. Allergies tend to appear according to their method of entry into

Photo Courtesy of
Gerry Cronin

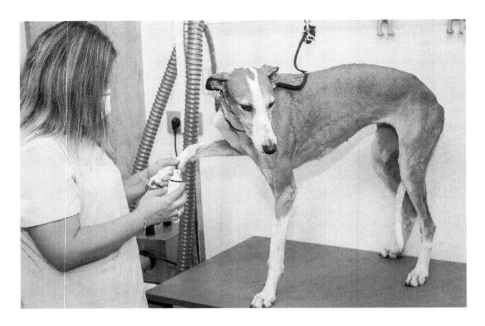

the body. The most common symptom is itching, which can be either generalized or localized. Coughing, sneezing, and watery eyes are also common symptoms. Dogs with food allergies may also experience vomiting or diarrhea. With food allergies, itching tends to be more generalized, but they may also develop yeast infections in specific parts of the body, such as the ears or paws. Dogs with allergies to plants or insects typically display symptoms such as itching, swelling, and redness on the area of the body that was exposed to the allergen. Inhaled allergens, such as pollen, can also cause respiratory problems such as wheezing, sneezing, coughing, or difficulty breathing.

Canine allergies are not an easy problem to diagnose or treat. Treatment tends to be more successful once the allergen is known, but narrowing down the allergen can be difficult, and testing is not always accurate. It can take weeks or even months for your veterinarian to determine a potential cause for your Greyhounds symptoms, so it's important to remain patient. Dogs are generally exposed to so many potential allergens in their environment that determining which one is the problem can be challenging.

In most cases, allergies are relatively simple to treat once the allergen is determined, but in some cases, the immune system's reaction may be so severe that the symptoms are more difficult to control. Injectable and oral antihistamines tend to produce the best results for environmental allergies. Medicated shampoos, conditioners, and ointments can help soothe irritated skin, but this is rarely a permanent solution. Dogs with food allergies may need to be fed specific diets to avoid certain proteins. As discussed in the chapter on nutrition, hypoallergenic diets may also be required.

In most cases, allergies are not life-threatening, but they can cause your Greyhound serious discomfort and distress. If your dog is displaying symptoms of allergies, it's best to consult your veterinarian as soon as possible to begin treatment and provide your Greyhound with relief. However, if your Greyhound is displaying symptoms of a more serious allergic reaction, such as trouble breathing, you need to seek veterinary care immediately.

Fleas and Ticks

It's not uncommon for dogs to pick up fleas and ticks from their environment, but it's important to seek treatment as soon as possible to prevent your dog from contracting dangerous diseases carried by these parasites. Thankfully, Greyhounds have short coats that make identifying external parasites a relatively simple job, so long as you keep an eye out.

Fleas and ticks are capable of carrying an array of diseases, some of which can be transferred to humans, so it's crucial to seek treatment as soon as possible to keep your entire family safe. Fleas often carry tapeworms or bartonellosis and can cause anemia. Many dogs experience flea allergy dermatitis, which causes serious itching, skin irritation, and even hair loss. The diseases carried by ticks vary by species and location, but possibilities include Lyme disease, babesiosis, Rocky Mountain spotted fever, and ehrlichiosis.

Prevention is the best medicine when it comes to parasites. There are many different flea and tick prevention products on the market, so it's best to ask your veterinarian to recommend a product based on where you live and the parasites present in that area. Depending on your location, you may need to apply preventative products year-round or just during the warmer seasons. Additionally, if you board your Greyhound frequently, your boarding facility may require your dog to be up to date on flea and tick prevention before being allowed to stay with them.

While flea and tick collars are an option, they are not recommended for most dogs. Many collars contain a chemical called tetrachlorvinphos, which is considered carcinogenic by the Environmental Protection Agency. It can cause serious reactions, including hair loss, skin irritation, diarrhea, and vomiting. More serious reactions such as seizures and death are also possible. Cats appear to be more sensitive to this chemical than dogs, so even if your cat isn't wearing the collar, it could come into contact with the medication just from interacting with your Greyhound.

Internal Parasites

It's not uncommon for Greyhounds of all ages to contract internal parasites, but the risk is often higher for puppies. Puppies often contract parasites from their mother or from simply exploring their environment with their mouths. Parasites are typically contracted when a dog consumes contaminated water, food, soil, or feces. Left untreated, internal parasites can cause serious health problems, and some zoonotic parasites may also be transferred to humans.

The most common intestinal worms that affect dogs are roundworms, hookworms, tapeworms, and whipworms, though there are many more that are possible, depending on the area you live in. Additionally, your Greyhound may also be at risk of ingesting protozoa such as giardia or coccidia, which can also cause serious illness.

Unfortunately, intestinal worms are not the only internal parasites you need to worry about. As the name suggests, heartworms are a parasite that infects the bloodstream and heart. They are transmitted by mosquitos, which spread them from host to host as they feed. Heartworms are generally considered to be more dangerous than intestinal worms because, when left untreated, they can permanently damage your Greyhound's heart and other vital organs.

Additionally, treatment can take many months and requires the dog to remain on kennel rest for the duration. This is because as the worms are killed off by treatment, strenuous physical activity can cause the blood to pump hard enough to cause the dead and dying parasites to block vital arteries. Without treatment, heartworm disease can be fatal, but it is preventable with a monthly chewable tablet that you can purchase from your veterinarian.

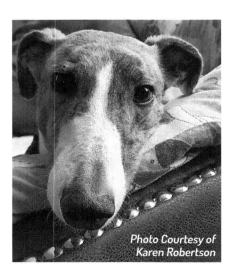

Photo Courtesy of Karen Robertson

Not all dogs infected with intestinal worms or heartworms will display symptoms, so it's important to have your dog tested at his annual checkups. However, common symptoms may include sudden weight loss, lethargy, coughing, vomiting, and diarrhea. It's common for dogs with heavy loads of parasites to appear malnourished but with a distended stomach. Many dogs with severe infections are also anemic.

If you believe that your Greyhound may be infected with heartworms, protozoa, or intestinal worms, it's important to seek veterinary care as soon as possible. Your vet will be able to test for parasites, which is a simple and inexpensive procedure. For intestinal parasites, a fecal sample is required. Your vet will be able to see eggs, larvae, and adult parasites under the microscope and prescribe treatment based on the specific types of parasite present.

Since heartworms infect the bloodstream, a blood sample is required for diagnosis. The blood is then mixed with a chemical solution and poured into a disposable device. The testing device must then be allowed to sit for several minutes, after which results will be readable. Generally, treatment is relatively simple and may involve injectable or oral medication. However, depending on the type of parasite, treatment may take between a few days to several months to complete.

Vaccinations

Throughout your Greyhound's life, he will periodically need to be vaccinated. The vaccines he needs will depend on several factors, including his age, lifestyle, and where you live. Vaccines are generally considered to be either core or non-core. Core vaccines include rabies, distemper, and parvovirus. These vaccines are given to all dogs and may even be required by law in some areas. Non-core vaccines, such as Bordetella and leptospirosis, have a shorter efficacy period and are not necessarily required in most areas.

Core vaccines are generally required by law because they protect dogs against some of the most common and dangerous diseases. Viruses such as rabies can be transmitted to humans, so it's essential to make sure the animals we share our homes with are protected. The rabies vaccine is required by law in the United States and must be administered by a licensed veterinarian. Additionally, it cannot be administered to dogs less than 16 weeks of age. Typically, the first rabies vaccine is only good for one year, but subsequent boosters may be given every three years after that.

The other core vaccine is called DHPP, which protects against distemper, parvovirus, parainfluenza, hepatitis, and adenovirus cough. As a puppy, your Greyhound will have received DHPP vaccines at six, twelve, and sixteen weeks of age. Adult dogs are typically given the vaccine every one to three years, depending on local laws and the veterinarian's recommendation.

Some DHPP vaccines may include protection against other diseases such as canine coronavirus or leptospirosis.

Non-core vaccines protect against less commonly encountered diseases and may vary by location. These vaccines often are not effective for as long of a period of time as core vaccines. Whereas the rabies vaccine may be good for up to three years, the Bordetella vaccine is only good for six months. Other examples of non-core vaccines include leptospirosis, Lyme disease, and rattlesnake venom. Though these vaccines are not required by law, Bordetella may be required by groomers and boarding facilities to protect from the highly contagious kennel cough.

Although allergic reactions to vaccines are rare, they are possible. To avoid potential reactions from their Greyhound's immune system, some owners choose to administer one vaccine at a time. For example, if your dog is due for both rabies and DHPP, you might choose to do rabies first and then DHPP a few weeks later. Though this will not completely eliminate the possibility of a reaction, it can help avoid overwhelming your dog's immune system.

Common symptoms of an allergic reaction include swelling of the face or paws, lethargy, hives, and vomiting. Less severe symptoms may include swelling or pain at the injection site. Severe reactions are rare, but they may include seizures and difficulty breathing. If you aren't sure how your Greyhound will react to vaccines, you might consider staying in the vicinity of your vet for 20 to 30 minutes after the injection. That way, if your Greyhound does react badly, immediate medical intervention is within reach.

If your Greyhound is sensitive to vaccines, or you don't want to risk over vaccinating him, you might also consider titer testing. In many areas, titer testing is a legal alternative to yearly core vaccines. The tests are performed by taking a blood sample and testing it for antibodies. If the antibodies are at adequate levels, your Greyhound will not need to be vaccinated at that time. If the levels are too low, he will require a vaccination to ensure that he's fully protected. Titer testing can be expensive in some areas and is generally not available for non-core vaccines, but for many sensitive Greyhounds, it is a safer alternative.

Spaying and Neutering

If you have rescued an adult Greyhound, he may already be spayed or neutered, which means you can avoid having to make choices regarding your dog's reproductive health. However, if you've brought home a puppy or unaltered adult, you'll need to decide when and if you want to spay or neuter. Spaying and neutering are surgical procedures that essentially remove the dog's reproductive organs, rendering the dog sterile and unable to reproduce.

For most pet owners, spaying and neutering relieves them of the responsibility of preventing unwanted pregnancies, whether in their own dogs or those they may come into contact with. If your Greyhound is a conformation show prospect, you will need to keep him intact as altered dogs are not allowed to compete. Altered dogs are allowed to compete in other sports, however, so spaying and neutering does not mean the end of your dog's career.

Unfortunately, the decision of whether to spay or neuter your Greyhound is not clear-cut. Most vets recommend alteration simply because it's easier for most people to manage their dogs if they don't have to worry about accidental breeding. However, there is an increasing amount of research that suggests that these procedures aren't the right choice for every dog. In some areas of the world, such as Norway, it's illegal to spay or neuter your dog if it's not for health reasons. It is often said that surgical sterilization reduces the risk of certain cancers, such as testicular or ovarian, but it's obviously difficult to develop cancer in body parts that are removed. Other types of cancer have a higher rate in altered dogs, and many studies show an increased rate of aggression in dogs that have been sterilized. However, research is ongoing and remains somewhat inconclusive about whether pet owners should definitively sterilize their dogs.

One conclusion revealed by this research is the dangers of spaying or neutering dogs too early. Studies have shown that dogs that have been altered at a young age are at a higher risk of orthopedic disorders such as hip dysplasia and canine cruciate ligament rupture. The reason for this is that the reproductive organs are responsible for the production of certain hormones that affect growth. Previously, the standard recommendation was to surgically sterilize dogs by the age of six months, but new research is suggesting that owners wait until dogs are fully grown at around 18 to 24 months for breeds as large as Greyhounds.

If you're interested in preserving your Greyhound's hormones without the risk of accidental litters, you may want to explore alternative procedures such as vasectomies and ovary sparing spays (OSS). A vasectomy is a surgical procedure that allows male dogs to keep their testicles, but the spermatic cord is transected so that the dog is no longer fertile. Ovary-sparing spays remove the uterus and cervix but leave the ovaries to continue producing necessary hormones.

If you're struggling to decide when and if you need to spay or neuter your Greyhound, discuss the matter with your veterinarian.

Holistic Alternatives

As more people seek a more natural lifestyle for themselves, it's not uncommon for them to desire the same type of care for their pets. Depending on where you live, you may be able to find a holistic veterinary clinic to provide care for your Greyhound. For those unfamiliar with holistic medical care, there is a common misconception that it consists only of treatments such as herbal remedies and acupuncture, but holistic veterinary care actually uses both conventional and alternative therapies to treat health issues. In fact, holistic veterinarians attend the same universities as more traditional vets and provide the same types of treatment. Where more traditional treatments fall short, holistic veterinarians are able to seek solutions in alternative therapies such as chiropractic care, acupuncture, and nutritional therapy.

The main difference between traditional and holistic veterinary care is that holistic vets treat the body as a whole rather than a series of individual parts. For example, if a dog has skin problems, a traditional vet may treat the issue with a series of topical ointments or injectable or oral medications. A holistic vet may try to improve the dog's overall health by addressing other aspects such as diet or lifestyle, in addition to more traditional treatments.

Photo Courtesy of
Paula Lawson

The goal is to improve the dog's overall health and treat the problem at its source rather than just address the symptoms. Many pets with chronic health problems may see improvement when alternative treatments are used.

If you're not sure where to find a holistic veterinarian, your best option is to consult the American Holistic Veterinary Medical Association's website. Their website lists holistic vets in the US and Canada and is searchable by species and specialty.

Pet Insurance

As with human health care, the cost of veterinary care continues to rise, and pet owners are constantly looking for ways to help mitigate the costs of keeping their beloved companions healthy. There are many companies offering insurance policies at different price points and levels of coverage. Unfortunately, there is no one plan that will suit all dogs, so it's important to thoroughly research plans to make sure your Greyhound has the coverage he needs. As with human insurance plans, older dogs and those with preexisting conditions may cost more to insure.

It's important to note that pet insurance typically only covers emergency care rather than preventative care. Annual exams, parasite prevention, and vaccinations will still require out-of-pocket payment, but if your Greyhound suddenly becomes ill or suffers an injury, your policy should cover the bulk of your expenses. A few companies do offer policies that cover preventative care, but those plans can be quite expensive.

When it comes to pet insurance, you need to consider the cost of your monthly premium and decide whether the benefits are worth it to you. Some owners swear by pet insurance as they have reaped the benefits of their policies. Others may be more dissatisfied from paying a monthly premium and having a healthy dog that doesn't require emergency care. Rather than committing to that monthly premium, some owners choose to set aside a certain amount of money each month as savings that they can rely on in an emergency. Only you can decide whether pet insurance is appropriate for you and your Greyhound, but it's crucial that you explore all of your options to ensure you make the right choice.

CHAPTER 18
Health Concerns in Greyhounds

In general, Greyhounds are a healthy breed, but as with all breeds, there are a few issues that Greyhounds are prone to developing. Unfortunately, not all problems can be predicted, but genetic testing allows owners and

Photo Courtesy of
Karen Nelson

Photo Courtesy of
Amy King

breeders to eliminate or reduce the chances of their dogs developing certain disorders. For breeders, in particular, genetic testing allows them to improve the Greyhound breed as a whole with each generation, potentially eliminating certain diseases from the gene pool. For this reason, if you are buying a Greyhound from a breeder, it's important to seek out reputable breeders rather than those who choose to forgo testing in order to make the most money.

Genetic testing is a simple process that begins with the collection of a dog's blood or saliva. The sample is then sent to a laboratory for proper analysis. Once the results are available, a breeder is able to determine whether they should include that individual dog in their breeding program, or if it's best to spay or neuter the dog and put him in a pet home. Reputable breeders never hide the results of genetic testing and typically submit their results to the Canine Health Information Center, where they can be made publicly available. In fact, the Orthopedic Foundation for Animals requires Greyhound breeders to submit a blood sample to participate in the OFA/CHIC DNA repository in order for their results to be publicly listed on the CHIC website.

Gastric Dilatation Volvulus or Bloat

Bloat is a serious condition that is common in deep-chested breeds such as the Greyhound. It occurs when the stomach fills with gas, food, or fluids. The expansion of the stomach puts increased pressure on other organs and can reduce blood flow. There is also an increased risk of the stomach wall tearing, and it can make it difficult for the dog to breathe. Bloat may also be caused by a condition known as gastric dilatation volvulus (GDV), which is when the stomach itself twists or rotates. GDV can stop blood flow to the stomach, which will cause a dog to go into shock. Left untreated, GDV is fatal.

Symptoms of bloat or GDV include restlessness, drooling, a distended stomach, weakness, and attempting to vomit. Affected dogs may also be short of breath, have a rapid heartbeat or pale gums, and collapse. If you believe that your Greyhound may be affected by this condition, it's important to seek treatment immediately. Depending on the severity of the situation, surgery may be required for survival.

Though bloat cannot entirely be prevented, there are a few steps you can take to reduce your dog's risk. Feeding dogs smaller meals throughout the day, rather than one large meal is recommended with breeds prone to bloat. You should also limit activity for a few hours before and after each meal. If your dog tends to gulp large amounts of water, you may need to limit his water so that he can only drink small amounts at a time. If your dog has not yet been spayed or neutered, you may also ask your veterinarian about stomach tacking, which is when the stomach is surgically tacked to the abdominal wall to prevent it from flipping.

HELPFUL TIP
Bone Cancer

One of the more severe health predispositions affecting Greyhounds is bone cancer or osteosarcoma. This aggressive bone cancer will typically affect one leg and presents as lameness. With early detection and aggressive treatment, cancer can sometimes be managed through amputation and chemotherapy but is otherwise fatal. Therefore, if your Greyhound develops a limp, schedule a visit with your veterinarian as soon as possible.

Osteosarcoma

One of the most common types of cancer to affect Greyhounds, osteosarcoma is diagnosed in Greyhounds at a much higher rate than in other breeds, though Great Danes and Rottweilers also have high rates. Osteosarcoma is unusual in that it affects dogs of all ages, but the risk does increase with age. In a study performed in the UK, it was estimated that osteosarcoma

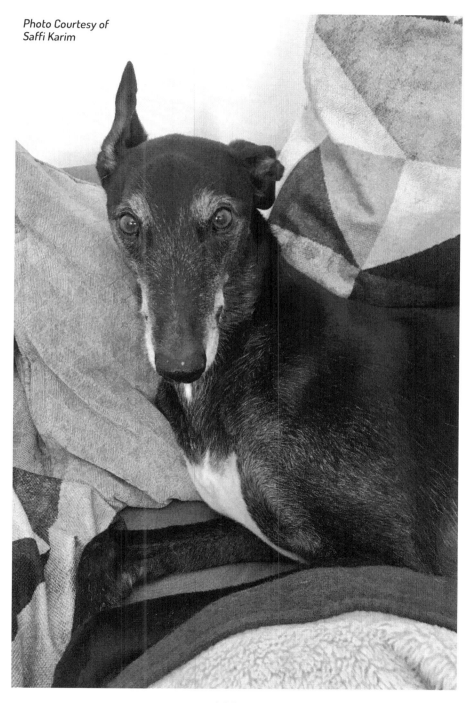

*Photo Courtesy of
Saffi Karim*

accounts for nearly half of all tumors in Greyhounds. It is most commonly seen in the front leg between the shoulder and wrist and in the hind leg around the stifle.

Symptoms of osteosarcoma include lameness and swelling or pain around the affected area. It can appear quickly, so many owners assume injury rather than cancer. The only way to properly diagnose osteosarcoma is through x-rays. X-rays frequently show that the affected area appears different from surrounding bone and may have an almost "moth-eaten" appearance. Osteosarcoma also frequently causes the bone to fracture, which accounts for the most painful cases.

Unfortunately, bone cancer is an incredibly aggressive disease and can spread quickly throughout the body. Unlike other types of cancer, osteosarcoma tends to spread early on, which means it's often progressed to other parts of the body by the time it's diagnosed. Most affected dogs have a poor prognosis and may have an estimated life expectancy of as little as a few months. Treatment options may include chemotherapy, radiotherapy, amputation, and pain-relieving medication. However, few dogs receiving treatment have a life expectancy longer than about 10 to 12 months.

Skin Problems

Greyhounds are prone to skin issues because of their thin skin and sparse coat. One benefit of their thin coat is that skin issues are easier to spot early on, which means treatment can be prescribed at an earlier stage. Possible skin conditions that can affect Greyhounds include blackheads, sunburn, fungal infections, and nail bed inflammation. Greyhounds are also prone to a unique condition called balding thighs. Though the cause of this condition is unknown, the result is a Greyhound with no hair on the backs of his thighs. Treatment for skin conditions will depend on the exact issue but generally are not complicated so long as the condition is caught and addressed in its early stages.

Regular monitoring of the skin and frequent grooming can help prevent skin problems and aid in early diagnosis. Additionally, if your Greyhound has balding thighs or just a sparse coat in certain areas, you may want to consider protecting him from the elements. It's not uncommon for Greyhounds to wear sweaters or coats in the winter and sun shirts or sunscreen in the summer. If you have any concerns about your Greyhound's skin or coat, it's important to ask your veterinarian as soon as possible.

Medication Sensitivities

Greyhounds have a well-documented sensitivity to certain types of medication, particularly anesthetic drugs. Anesthetics such as thiopental and propofol can result in prolonged recovery from surgical procedures. The reason for this is that Greyhounds, as well as some other sighthounds, are deficient in the hepatic enzyme responsible for the metabolism of these types of drugs. Thiopental is no longer commercially available in the United States, but propofol is still widely used for a variety of procedures.

It's also been suggested that Greyhounds and other sighthounds may be more sensitive to lipophilic drugs, such as anesthetics, due to their low body fat. As these drugs require fatty tissue to metabolize, it's understandable that this would be more difficult on leaner breeds such as the Greyhound.

Though most veterinarians are well-versed in the use of anesthetics in sighthounds, it's worth mentioning if your Greyhound is scheduled for any procedure requiring anesthesia. Again, if you have any additional questions or concerns regarding your Greyhound's experiences with anesthesia, always ask your vet. Most vets would much rather address an owner's concerns upfront rather than have them fretting while their beloved companion is anesthetized.

Preventing Illnesses

Unfortunately, no matter how well we take care of our Greyhounds, we cannot entirely prevent them from falling ill. However, proper management of your dog's health, nutrition, and lifestyle will ensure that he lives as long and happy of a life as possible. By bringing an animal into your home, you're accepting this responsibility for the life of the animal.

One of the best ways to help prevent your Greyhound from developing serious illnesses is to make sure he sees a vet on a regular basis for checkups. By taking your dog to the vet every six to twelve months, you're more likely to catch serious conditions early enough to provide treatment. Additionally, those frequent visits allow you the opportunity to ask your vet questions that may not seem serious enough to warrant their own vet visit but could affect your dog's health over time. Questions about diet, weight, fitness, or behavior often fall in this category. Additionally, regular preventative visits will help keep your Greyhound up to date on all vaccinations and parasite prevention.

CHAPTER 19
The Aging Greyhound

Basics of Senior Dog Care

The Greyhound is a large breed of dog, which means they're typically considered to be seniors when they reach approximately seven years of age. This doesn't necessarily mean that your Greyhound will require different care beginning the morning of his seventh birthday, but it does mean this is the approximate age at which he will begin to slow down. Not all dogs age at the same rate, so your dog may begin to display signs of old age when he's five, or he may not start slowing down until he's nine. As with humans, aging is different between individuals, and even if you have two Greyhounds of the same age, they may age in completely different ways or at different rates.

Photo Courtesy of
Margaret Robart
Picture by Chris Robart

The signs of aging may also appear so slowly that you don't necessarily recognize them at first. You see your Greyhound every day, so it can be hard to notice subtle changes in his appearance or behavior. The early signs of aging often include sleeping more during the day, getting tired more quickly during physical activities, and struggling to get out of bed or up stairs. Many older Greyhounds also begin losing their hearing or vision, so it's important to be careful around your senior dog to avoid startling him. Weight change is also a common occurrence with older dogs due to changes in metabolism. This can result in aging dogs that put on a few extra pounds or dogs that become quite thin.

HELPFUL TIP
In Loving Memory

When it's time to say goodbye to your beloved Greyhound, you may be searching for a way to preserve his memory. One option is to make a donation to the Greyhound Gang, a 501c3 organization that has been "dedicated to the rescue, rehabilitation, and adoption of Greyhounds" since 1995. Your dog's image will be displayed on the organization's "In Memory" webpage, and the donation will go towards the organization's operating costs. For more information, visit www. greyhoundgang.org.

Older Greyhounds often require more frequent trips outside, as they no longer have the same control over their bladder that they used to. One of the most difficult symptoms of aging in any dog is cognitive dysfunction or dementia. Cognitive dysfunction often presents as changes in behavior or temporary confusion, so it's important to be patient with your Greyhound during these periods. The more you notice these changes in your Greyhound, the more you'll need to adapt his care and lifestyle to his changing needs.

Regular Vet Visits

As your Greyhound ages, you may find that you will need to visit your vet more frequently. It's not uncommon for vets to recommend twice-yearly checkups rather than the usual once yearly for young dogs. Since a dog's body changes rapidly as he ages, it's important to schedule more frequent checkups to ensure that any problems are addressed sooner rather than later. Many older dogs also experience a decline in dental health and may require more frequent dental cleanings in their golden years.

More frequent checkups will also allow you to bring up any concerns you may have about your Greyhound's aging body and mind. Many older Greyhounds can benefit from changes in diet or the addition of nutritional supplements or medications, especially if your dog is suffering from common conditions such as arthritis. Always remember to mention any sudden changes in weight or behavior with your veterinarian, and these can be early warning signs of a variety of health problems.

Nutritional Changes

It's uncommon for Greyhounds to enter into their senior years without a significant change in nutrition required by their changing bodies. Though active adult Greyhounds may be able to eat high-calorie foods without gaining an ounce, older dogs typically do not have that luxury, and steps must be taken to ensure they maintain a healthy weight. Obesity can cause health problems at any age, but it's especially serious for older dogs who may be battling other conditions such as arthritis. The pain from arthritis can reduce mobility, which can cause weight gain if the dog's diet is not addressed. Even if you don't change your Greyhound's food, you will need to adjust his portion sizes. You may also consider switching your Greyhound to a food formulated specifically for seniors. These types of food tend to contain fewer calories and may also contain increased fiber or joint support.

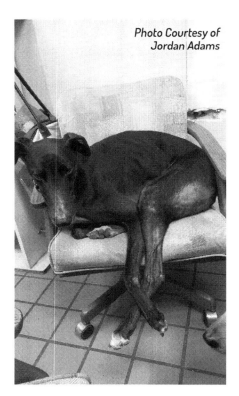

Photo Courtesy of Jordan Adams

If your Greyhound appears to be losing weight, there are several things you can do to help him maintain a healthy weight. Weight loss is a common occurrence with aging dogs. Some may simply be experiencing changes in their metabolism, while others may struggle with their appetite. Sometimes the solution to this problem is as simple as changing food or adding toppers to their meal. Seniors with dental problems may simply need a softer food. However, before changing your senior Greyhound's diet, schedule a checkup with your vet to make sure your dog isn't losing weight for other reasons.

Aging Greyhounds may also develop any number of health problems as they progress through their

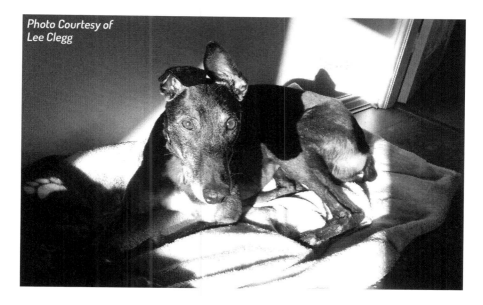

senior years. This can result in the need for nutritional changes. Dogs that develop issues with their heart or kidneys, for example, may require a prescription diet in order for them to maintain their health. For Greyhounds struggling with mobility, the addition of joint supplements such as glucosamine, chondroitin, MSM, or green-lipped mussel can make a world of difference. Seniors dealing with digestive issues may also benefit from additional fiber, probiotics, or digestive enzymes in their diet. Again, before adding any supplements to your Greyhound's diet, be sure to discuss the matter with your vet to make sure it's the best option for your dog.

Exercising Your Senior Dog

As your Greyhound ages, you'll also need to adjust his exercise schedule to accommodate his changing body and energy levels. As dogs get older, their exercise needs typically decrease, which means your Greyhound may have less stamina or enthusiasm for activities he once enjoyed. Many older Greyhounds spend more time snoozing on the sofa than they did in their youth. However, it's important not to completely eliminate exercise from your senior Greyhound's daily schedule. Exercise is crucial to good health, but you may need to reduce the length of his walks or look for other opportunities such as swimming.

If your Greyhound's body no longer allows him to feel fulfilled with his shortened daily exercise routine, you may want to consider substituting more mental challenges into his schedule. Mentally stimulating activities are a great way to keep your Greyhound's mind active without overstressing his body. From puzzle toys to scentwork, there are plenty of opportunities to get your dog to use his brain more than his body.

To accommodate your Greyhound's changing body, you may also need to change his environment to help him exercise safely. Hard surfaces such as pavement can be hard on aging joints, as can difficult challenges such as stairs. This can increase your Greyhound's risk of injuring himself during activities. Rather than his usual walk around the neighborhood sidewalks, consider walking him through a grassy park or dirt trail if there are any in your area. Softer surfaces will be easier on your Greyhound's joints, and the change in scenery will help to keep his mind active and engaged.

Photo Courtesy of
Blazka Ribic

Environmental Changes

As previously mentioned, it's important to change your Greyhound's environment to suit his aging body, but this applies to your home as well as your walking route. Many older dogs lose strength and cannot recover as easily should they lose their footing. Slick flooring such as tile or hardwood can become a challenge to older Greyhounds as they can slip and fall more easily. You may want to consider investing in a few new rugs for your home to help your dog keep his footing as he travels through the house. It may also be a good idea to install temporary baby gates near stairs to ensure that your Greyhound doesn't accidentally take a tumble.

If you aren't willing to place rugs throughout your home, you can also have your dog wear nonslip booties or socks. If your Greyhound sleeps on the furniture, you may want to add steps for easier access or provide him with lower alternatives. Many older dogs are happy to give up their spot on the sofa once they have their own comfortable bed on the floor. Additionally, if you live in a home with long flights of stairs, you can also purchase special types of harnesses that allow owners to assist their Greyhounds in climbing or descending safely.

It's not uncommon for aging Greyhounds to experience cognitive dysfunction or confusion, so you may need to take steps to keep your companion safe. This also applies to dogs that may be losing their eyesight. Stairs, pools, and uneven surfaces can pose a danger to an older dog, especially one that may be confused or going blind. Limiting your Greyhound's access to these areas could potentially save his life. If your Greyhound is losing his hearing, you may need to take extra precautions to ensure that he doesn't escape your home. A deaf Greyhound might not be able to hear potential dangers such as cars if he were to suddenly find himself in the middle of the street. Though many of the changes in this section may require you to alter your home's décor, it's important to prioritize the comfort and safety of your aging Greyhound.

Preparing to Say Goodbye

There will come a time in every Greyhound's life where you will need to say goodbye. In many cases, this time comes sooner than we may expect, so it's important to have a plan. As your Greyhound ages, you will need to prioritize his quality of life and be prepared to intervene when he no longer enjoys his favorite activities and his moments of suffering outnumber his moments of joy. It can be difficult to determine when it's time to say goodbye, but using a quality-of-life scale, such as the one developed by veterinary oncologist Dr. Alice Villalobos, can be helpful. Dr. Villalobos' scale suggests evaluating each of the seven aspects of quality-of-life on a scale of 1 to 10. If the overall score is less than 35, humane euthanasia is recommended. The seven categories are:

- Hurt
- Hunger
- Hydration
- Hygiene
- Happiness
- Mobility
- More Good Days Than Bad

In some cases, there may be alternatives to euthanasia that you may choose to improve your Greyhound's quality of life. Items on the list, such as hygiene and mobility, are connected, so when a dog's mobility is improved through the use of a canine wheelchair or surgical procedure, his ability to relieve himself cleanly also improves. Changes in diet can improve hunger and hydration, while medication can improve both hurt and mobility. However, other items such as happiness may not always improve if others are addressed. If you're struggling to decide how to judge your Greyhound's quality of life, your veterinarian will be able to advise you on the appropriate time to say goodbye.

While some Greyhounds do pass away peacefully in their sleep, it's more likely that you will need to assist your companion over the Rainbow Bridge through humane euthanasia. Euthanasia is a painless procedure that ensures that your Greyhound does not suffer. This procedure is performed by your vet, who administers a lethal overdose of a drug called sodium pentobarbital. The drug is injected into the dog's vein, typically in one of the front legs. In many cases, the dog is sedated before this injection to further relax him, especially if the dog is confused or in pain. For most dogs, having their beloved owner by their side can help them relax and understand that it's okay to go. It takes only seconds for the sodium pentobarbital to begin taking effect, and the heart typically stops in less than a minute. Your veterinarian will be able to confirm that the heart has stopped with a stethoscope.

In your Greyhound's final moments, it's understandable that you may be overcome with grief and unable to make important decisions. This is why it's important to consider these things in advance if possible. Some veterinary clinics offer both in-home and in-clinic euthanasia, so you can choose where you want to say goodbye. Some owners would simply prefer to say goodbye in the privacy of their own home, while others may not want those painful memories to take place there. If you have the opportunity, consider discussing your options with your vet so that arrangements can be made in advance. Wherever you choose to say goodbye, your Greyhound will be comforted by knowing that he is surrounded by family in his final moments.

Saying goodbye is not the final decision you must make during this stressful time. You must also decide what to do with your Greyhound's remains. Your veterinarian will be able to provide you with several options, including cremation. If you would prefer not to have your companion's remains returned to you, most vets are able to respectfully take care of the remains for you. If you have the opportunity to explore these options in advance, you may be able to make a plan with your veterinarian so that when the time comes, you are able to focus on saying goodbye rather than dealing with these decisions.

Grief and Healing

The grieving period after losing your beloved Greyhound will be difficult but understand that it will get easier. Everyone who has ever been blessed with sharing their lives with a dog understands the pain that you're experiencing. You are not alone. During this challenging time, it may be helpful for you to reach out to friends or family for comfort. If you have other pets in your home, be sure to shower them with love and let them know how much you appreciate them being in your life.

You may also want to consider memorializing your Greyhound's life. Various artists and companies offer a range of personalized memorials, including jewelry, garden décor, and ceramic tiles for you to remember your Greyhound by. If you'd like your Greyhound's memory to benefit others, consider donating to a Greyhound rescue group or local animal shelter. You can also plant trees or gardens in your community. If you have the time, volunteering in your community is also a great way of navigating by your grief through helping others in need.

It's essential that you understand that what you are feeling is normal. Everyone experiences grief differently, and some people may struggle more than others. If you are struggling to cope with your feelings, consider reaching out to a grief counselor or mental health professional. Not everyone possesses the coping skills to deal with such a tragic loss, and a professional may be able to help you process your feelings more easily. However you choose to process your grief and healing, don't forget to cherish the memories of your beloved Greyhound. Remember, you provided him with the same unconditional love that he gave to you.

Made in the USA
Coppell, TX
26 November 2022

87091324R00090